UNFIT FOR SALE

UNFIT FOR SALE

அறம்

Siva Murugan B

Reclaiming Masculinity Through Ancient Tamizh Wisdom

ISBN: 978-93-5659-893-5

This is a work of nonfiction. The views and reflections expressed in this book are those of the author. References to people, events, or situations are intended for illustrative or philosophical purposes only. Any resemblance to actual persons or events is coincidental.

This book is not intended as legal, financial, or medical advice. Readers are encouraged to exercise their own judgment.

Interior arts by: Siva Murugan B
First Edition — 2026

For more writings, visit:
www.sivamurugan.co.in

For inquiries, permissions, or feedback, please contact:
future.is.now.siva5101999@gmail.com

DEDICATION

To my parents, my brother & my relatives,
for their sacrifice, patience, and quiet strength.

And to my ancestors of the Chera & Pandya land,
and the teachers of the Tamizh tradition,
whose wisdom continues to guide my steps.

And finally, to my Gurus for trusting
an atheist like me and accepting me as their disciple,
particularly Sivan, Parvati, and Sivavakkiyar,
whose presence and grace guide me on this journey of life.

TO WHOM THIS BOOK?

This book is not about the outer game. It is not a manual for winning the races you have already grown tired of running. This book is for the moment after the applause fades, when you have secured the safety, achieved the comfort, and felt the hollow weight of a trophy that cannot fill the silence within. It is for when you realize the unconditional love you seek from another can only be built upon the unconditional integrity you offer to yourself. The deepest betrayal is not by another, but by your own refusal to stand for your soul, a crime that leaves your heart lost, with nowhere to cry.

While framed for men, this is not exclusive. It's for any woman who recognizes that the journey from seeking validation in the world's mirror to finding authority in your own heart is a universal passage.

The journey hinges on a reordering of the self: **Mind < Heart < Soul.**

Your mind calculates and manages to ensure you do not get hurt. Your soul knows your deepest truth, an aspect the mind cannot explore on its own. Your heart, however, acts as the intermediary that communicates with both soul and mind. You can possess everything your mind was taught to want, **yet if your heart is ignored, it has its own way of punishing you. It will answer with a quiet, relentless sadness.** When you finally choose your soul's direction, even without permission, your heart feels a profound peace: **"Finally, you are here for me."**

This book is an invitation to that reunion. It is a call to look past the noise of what you should want and to begin a quiet dialogue with what you truly value. It offers a map built on ancient wisdom to reclaim the sixteen forms of wealth that cannot be bought, sold, or displayed: they can only be lived.

If you are ready to move beyond the chase and to question what you've been sold, then this is your companion. Turn the page. The real work begins within.

CONTENTS

CONTENTS

ஐந்துகரத்தனை ஆனை முகத்தனை
இந்தின் இளம்பிறைபோலும் எயிற்றனை
நந்தி மகன்தனை ஞானக் கொழுந்தினைப்
புந்தியில் வைத்தடி போற்றுகின் றேனே.

திருச்சிற்றம்பலம்!

நமசிவாய வாழ்க, நாதன் தாள் வாழ்க.
இமைப்பொழுதும் என் நெஞ்சில் நீங்காதான் தாள் வாழ்க.
கோகழி ஆண்ட குருமணிதன் தாள் வாழ்க.
ஆகமம் ஆகிநின்று அண்ணிப்பான் தாள் வாழ்க.
ஏகன், அநேகன், இறைவன் அடி வாழ்க.

பார்த்ததேது பார்த்திடில் பார்வையூ டழிந்திடும்,
கூத்ததாய் இருப்பிரேல் குறிப்பிலாச் சிவமதாம்.
பார்த்தபார்த்த போதெல்லாம் பார்வையுமிகந்துநீர்,
பூத்தபூவுங் காயுமாய் பொருந்துவீர் பிறப்பிலே.

— சிவவாக்கியர்

ஆதித்தீயன் வாழ்க.

வெற்றி வேல் வீர வேல்!!!

WAKE UP FROM THE DREAM

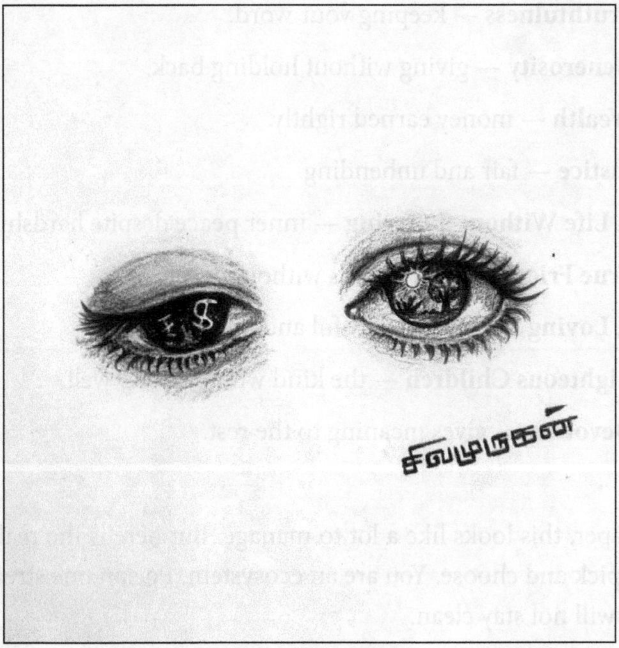

Most people think wealth is just a number on a screen. But we know, deep down, that's a lie. You can have a million in the bank and still feel like a bankrupt man if your life is a mess.

The ancient Tamizh texts had a much sharper handle on this. They didn't just talk about "money." They identified sixteen distinct forms of wealth. They didn't see them as a checklist, but as a **living system.**

1. **Wisdom** — the ability to think and live well.
2. **Beauty** — grace, inside and out.
3. **Strength** — of body and mind.

4. **Youthfulness** — a hunger for life.
5. **A Healthy Body** — free from illness.
6. **A Steady Mind** — a quiet, unshaken peace.
7. **A Good Name** — a reputation that lasts.
8. **Truthfulness** — keeping your word.
9. **Generosity** — giving without holding back.
10. **Wealth** — money earned rightly.
11. **Justice** — fair and unbending.
12. **A Life Without Suffering** — inner peace despite hardship.
13. **True Friendship** — friends without deceit.
14. **A Loving Partner** — faithful and kind.
15. **Righteous Children** — the kind who grow up well.
16. **Devotion** — gives meaning to the rest.

On paper, this looks like a lot to manage. But here is the reality. You cannot pick and choose. You are an ecosystem. Poison one stream, and the rest will not stay clean.

Imagine a man is offered a shortcut. It is a grey deal. Not a headline-making crime, just a subtle bending of the truth in a contract to pocket an extra twenty thousand dollars. In his head, he tells himself it is just business. It does not change who he is.

He is wrong. The moment that money hits his account, his brain undergoes a shift. First, his internal reward system is rewired. His mind has just learned that it can bypass months of steady discipline with a ten-minute lie. The next time a clean opportunity appears, it feels slow and inefficient. He has effectively doped his career. Now he needs the shortcut just to feel like he is winning. He can no longer stand for truth, because he has become dependent on the reward of the easy path.

Then the projection begins. Because he knows how easily he compromised his own integrity, he loses the ability to believe in anyone else's. When a business partner suggests a new strategy, he does not see trust or friendship. He sees a hidden agenda. He starts hearing double meanings in ordinary conversations. He stops looking clients in the eye, not out of guilt, but out of a growing belief that everyone is predatory. He has traded peace for a permanent state of quiet suspicion.

The most devastating ripple reaches his home.

He walks through the front door and looks at his wife, his loving partner. But because he has assigned a price to his own soul, he unconsciously assigns one to hers.

If I can be bought for twenty thousand, why wouldn't she be?

Her affection begins to feel transactional. When she asks how his day was, he does not hear care. He hears an audit. He starts to believe she is not there for him, but for the provider role he performs. He stops being vulnerable, because vulnerability is impossible with someone you experience as a creditor. By devaluing himself, he has made it impossible to truly value her. The wealth of partnership does not disappear because she changed. It disappears because he has lost the capacity to recognize unconditional love.

At three in the morning, he lies awake replaying the deal, scanning for the places he might get caught. To quiet his mind, he reaches for a drink. He wakes up with a heavy head and a shorter fuse. Health and vitality quietly erode.

He did not just tell a lie. He dropped a stone into the still water of his life. The ripples are now weakening the foundation of everything he claims to value. He traded a fortress of quiet, enduring wealth for a single bag of gold.

It is the most catastrophic trade a man can make.

Now, look at the flip side.

Imagine that same man says no to the crooked deal. He loses the contract. He drives home twenty thousand dollars poorer than he could have been. He feels the sting in his wallet, and let's be honest, it hurts. He is not a saint. He is a man who likes to win, and today he took a hit. But that night, something happens that money cannot buy.

Nothing.

There is no loop running in his head. There is no tightness in his shoulders. Because he did not cheat, he does not have to wonder who might be cheating him. His steady mind remains an asset, not a liability.

Because his mind is quiet, he is fully present at the dinner table. When his son talks about a problem at school, he is not nodding while secretly running calculations in his head. He is listening. He is investing in righteous children. He is not performing strength for his family. He is the strength.

Because he is not hiding a secret, he does not need to build walls. He looks at his wife, his loving partner, and he does not see someone to be managed. He sees a teammate. He can afford vulnerability because there is nothing to protect. The openness of the relationship remains intact because he has not poisoned his own capacity for trust.

He did not get richer that day, but he did something more profitable. He protected the infrastructure of his life. By refusing to pawn his truthfulness, he preserved his clarity of judgment and his good name. In doing so, **he made a quiet declaration that his self-respect is worth more than a twenty-thousand-dollar line item.**

And here is the part most people miss. Because his mind is steady and his reputation is clean, he is actually more likely to land the next hundred-thousand-dollar opportunity. He is playing the long game while others scramble for short-term wins in the grey.

Reminder: A man with a full bank account but a shaky mind and fake friends isn't "winning." He's just a high-net-worth disaster waiting to happen.

The Modern Trade-Off: Why We Keep Failing

If this system of sixteen riches is so logical, why are most of us broke in at least ten of them?

It's because we live in a culture of **hyper-specialization**. In the modern world, you are encouraged to be a "specialist." You're a specialist at your job, a specialist at your hobby, or a specialist at making money. But nobody teaches us how to be a specialist at living.

We've been conditioned to believe that life is a series of trades. We think:

- I'll sacrifice my health now so I can get the wealth.
- I'll ignore my partner while I build my reputation

We treat these sixteen forms of wealth like separate bank accounts, thinking we can overdraw one to fund another. But life doesn't have a currency exchange. You cannot buy back the "Righteous Children" you ignored for twenty years with the "Wealth" you earned while you were away. The math simply doesn't work.

Hidden Tax on Success

There is a hidden tax on every choice we make. When you choose to be a man who prizes dominance over justice, you pay a tax in "Steady Mind". When you choose a lifestyle that prioritizes flash over truthfulness, you pay a tax in "True Friendship".

Most men I know are exhausted not because they are working hard, but because they are tired of paying these taxes. They are tired of the "performance."

Think about the "Good Name". In the ancient sense, a good name wasn't about PR or a polished social media profile. It was about integrity—the idea that who you are in the dark is the same person you are in the light. Today, we spend so much energy managing our "reputation" that we have no energy left for our "character." We are building billboards for lives that are actually crumbling behind the sign.

The Keystone: Where to Start?

You might look at this list of sixteen and feel overwhelmed. It feels like trying to juggle sixteen glass balls at once. You're waiting for the sound of them shattering on the floor.

But here is the secret the ancient Tamizh poets understood: **You don't have to fix all sixteen at once.** In every man's life, there is a Keystone Wealth. A keystone is the stone at the top of an arch; if you set that one stone correctly, it holds the weight of all the others.

For some men, the keystone is Health. When they stop treating their body like a trash can and start moving again, their "Steady Mind" returns. Because they feel better, they are kinder to their "Partner".

For other men, the keystone is Truthfulness. The moment they stop lying—to their boss, to their spouse, to themselves—the "paranoia" vanishes. They suddenly have the "Wisdom" to see their path clearly because they aren't blinded by their own smoke and mirrors.

A 3:00 AM Audit

I'm not going to give you a "To-Do" list. That's just more work. Instead, I want you to do an audit.

Tonight, or the next time you find yourself staring at the ceiling at 3:00 AM when the world is quiet, ask yourself:

- **Which of the sixteen am I "pawning" right now?** What am I giving away for cheap just to keep my head above water?
- **Which one, if I fixed it, would make the others easier?** If I finally dealt with my "Steady Mind," would my "Wealth" actually grow because I'm making better decisions?
- What is the "cleanest" version of my life?

The Road Ahead

This book isn't a lecture. It's an invitation to stop building your life like a series of disconnected rooms and start seeing it as one single, beautiful architecture.

We're going to look at how we, as men, can stop "pawning" our peace of mind for things that don't satisfy us. We'll be honest about how hard it is, we'll laugh at our own mistakes, and we'll figure out how to keep the things that actually matter.

◆◆◆

We think masculinity is built on what we provide.
But its true foundation is why we provide.
Turn from the crowd, and you will meet your soul.

WHO PUT THE EVIL EYE ON US?

Most men get the "Provider" talk early in life. We're told our value is basically tied to being a human ATM. Feed the family, pay the mortgage, keep the lights on—that's the job.

And sure, that's part of it. But providing without **consciousness** is just a chore. It's robotic. The real weight of masculinity isn't just in the check you write; it's in the awareness you bring to the table.

Think about the last time you helped a neighbor fix a fence or picked up the tab for a friend who was struggling. When you did it without making a scene, it felt… solid. It felt natural. That's because giving is one of those sixteen forms of wealth. But somewhere along the line, we stopped giving to be helpful and started giving to be seen.

How did we get so twisted? It wasn't some grand conspiracy. We just started living in front of two mirrors.

The Two Mirrors

Masculinity was supposed to be a "net"—a safety net where if one guy is drowning, another reaches out. But the moment we start looking at ourselves instead of the guy in the water, the net breaks.

We all carry these two mirrors in our heads:

1. **The Social Mirror:** This is the imaginary crowd in your head. It wants points. It wants you to look like "The Man." It turns a simple act of help into a theatrical performance.
2. **The Thinking Mirror:** This is that internal voice that is constantly ranking you. "Does this make me look weak? Does this make me look richer than him?" It's obsessed with safety through status.

When these mirrors take over, you aren't "providing" anymore. You're just **marketing**. You aren't lifting someone up; you're standing on their shoulders so you can look taller.

Status vs. The Light

I remember being at a housewarming party a few years back. Two guys showed up with gifts, and the difference was a masterclass in these mirrors.

One guy, let's call him Ravi, walked in with a massive, shiny home theatre speaker. He did not just bring it. He announced it. He made sure everyone knew exactly how much bass it had and, implicitly, how much it cost. He was feeding his social mirror. He spent the rest of the night scanning the room to see if people were still impressed. He was giving, but what he was really doing was buying applause.

Then there was Murthy. He brought a simple, handmade clay lamp. He didn't make a speech. He just handed it over and said he thought it would look nice in the corner. The room didn't erupt in cheers. In fact, a few people probably thought it was a "cheap" gift.

But look at their faces. Ravi was on edge all night, making sure his "status" was intact. Murthy was relaxed. He was actually there at the party. He talked to people without scanning their faces for approval. He didn't need the room to tell him he was a good friend; he already knew. And if, even for a moment, he had started wondering what they might think of him, that ease would have vanished for him too.

The "Hidden Hook"

The person receiving it can feel the difference. They do not feel helped. They feel indebted. Instead of a bond, you have created a ledger. You begin expecting a return on your investment, not in cash, but in gratitude, in approval, or in being treated like the boss.

This is how a man loses his "True Friendship" and "Loving Partner" wealth. Nobody wants to be a character in your personal highlight reel. They want a partner, not a performer.

Taking the Mirrors Down

So, how do we stop performing and start providing? It's about putting the steering wheel back in your hands.

- **The "Chest Check"** Next time you are about to do something generous, pause. Feel the motive in your chest. Does it feel like sugar, a quick and hollow spike of vanity? Or does it feel like bread, a slow and steady sense that this is simply what needs to be done? If it is sugar, wait.
- **The Ghost Act** Try doing one genuinely helpful thing this week and tell absolutely no one. No photo. No casual mention to your wife. No story at the bar. Just do it and let it remain between you

and the universe. Notice the sting that comes from not receiving credit. That sting is your ego resisting. Let it pass.

- **Be Ruthless with the "Why"** If you're about to buy the "big gift" or make the "big gesture," ask yourself: "Would I still do this if I couldn't tell a single soul about it?" If the answer is no, you're serving the Social Mirror. Put the wallet away.
- **Strengthen the Net** Real masculinity is about strengthening the "village." If your buddy is losing his "Steady Mind," give him some of your time. If another guy is struggling with his "Good Name," offer him some wisdom. You aren't doing this to climb the rankings; you're doing it because if the net is strong, you're safer too.

The Driver in the Seat

A man who provides without consciousness is like a truck with a brick on the gas pedal and nobody at the wheel. It's moving, sure, but it's probably going to end up in a ditch.

We take the mirrors down because we want a full life, the sixteen forms of wealth. We want to be the kind of men who can sleep at night without checking our phones to see if the world approved of our day.

We provide because we can. We give because it's who we are. And we don't need a mirror to tell us we're enough.

◆ ◆ ◆

One man feeds the crowd's hunger for show.
Another feeds the quiet hunger for goodness.
The first is heard.
The second is felt.

WILL I BE EATEN ALIVE?

You finally decide to stop playing the game. You tell yourself, "I'm living for my own happiness now. I'm done performing for the crowd."

It feels great for about ten seconds. Then, that small, jagged voice in the back of your head starts chirping: "You're going to look weak. People are going to see you being 'kind' and they're going to eat you alive. You're basically inviting them to walk all over you."

That voice sounds like common sense. It sounds like survival. But it's just your **Thinking Mirror** doing its job.

The Thinking Mirror vs. The Social Mirror

We've already talked about the Social Mirror—the one that lives for the "likes" and the applause. But the Thinking Mirror is different. **It doesn't care if people clap; it just wants to make sure you don't get hurt.**

The Thinking Mirror is obsessed with "Safety through Drama." It hates grey areas. It likes to put everyone into two boxes: Predator or Prey. Winner or Loser. User or Used.

It tells you that if you aren't the one holding the whip, you must be the one feeling it. But there is a third state—a "quiet gear" that the mirror can't see because it isn't flashy: **Consciousness.**

The Mental Ledger vs. The Solid Floor

Most men aren't trying to be "show-offs." We are just trying not to get screwed over. When that "Thinking Mirror" starts whispering that you'll be eaten alive, it's inviting you to live your life by a Mental Ledger. This is the internal accountant who lives in your head, constantly checking the balance.

This man treats every interaction like a line item in a spreadsheet.

- *"I helped him with his car, so he owes me a favor."*
- *"I was the 'nice guy' today, so why didn't I get that promotion?"*

He's not necessarily a bad guy, but he is an exhausted one. He's always checking the math. Because he views his kindness as a "currency" he is spending, he's terrified of his account hitting zero. When someone doesn't "pay him back" with gratitude or a return favor, he feels a spike of panic. He feels like a "sucker."

He isn't building a life; he's just managing a debt collection agency in his own mind.

Now, look at the man who decides to build a Solid Floor. He doesn't view his actions as "spending" value; he views them as setting stones. When he chooses to be truthful, fair or generous, he isn't handing out coins and hoping for a return. He is pouring concrete under his own feet. He is making himself heavier, more stable, and harder to move.

He doesn't need to check the "Ledger" because his value doesn't come from what he gets back from people. It comes from the fact that he is standing on a floor he built himself. If someone is thankless, it doesn't "drain" him. You can't steal the floor from under a man who knows exactly why he placed every stone.

The Secret Invoice

The fear of being "used" usually comes from a lack of clarity. You have to stop lying to yourself about why you're helping. Before you do a favor, ask yourself: **"Am I expecting something in return?"**

- **If the answer is YES:** Stop trying to be a "saint." Just be a businessman. There is a clean, masculine dignity in a fair trade. Just say it: "I can help you with this for an hour, but I'm going to need your eyes on my report next week." Clarity lets everyone breathe. No "hidden hooks."
- **If the answer is NO:** Then give the help and, this is the hard part, delete the mental receipt. If you want it softer or more forceful, just say the word.

We add a column in our head called "They Owe Me." The other person senses it. Their "thank you" feels like an IOU. When they don't pay you back in the exact way you expected, you feel "used."

The Conscious Man

A "nice guy" often acts kindly because he wants approval, appreciation, or to be seen as good, which gives other people power over his emotions. A conscious man is different. He acts with intention, choosing kindness or firmness because it is right, not because he expects anything in return. Being "unusable" does not mean being rude or cold; it means he cannot be manipulated by praise, guilt, or rejection because he is not attached to other people's opinions. When he stops keeping score of who noticed, who thanked, or who owed him something, small slights lose their sting. His sense of stability comes from within, so careless remarks or lack of recognition no longer shake him.

How to start building the foundation:

- **The Motive Check:** Before you say "Yes," ask: "Is this a gift or a trade?"
- **Name the Trade:** Don't be "polite" and then bitter. If you need something back, say it. People prefer a clear deal over a "kindness" with a hidden bill.
- **The Ritual of Forgetting:** After you help someone, take one deep breath and tell yourself: "This is done." Erase the mental receipt. Don't let it take up space in your head.
- **Say 'No' Like a Man:** You aren't a 24/7 convenience store. If you can't give without feeling bitter, don't give. A clean "No" is better than a resentment-filled "Yes."

Will people think you're "weak" if you stop acting for the crowd? Maybe. Let the Thinking Mirror gossip. In the meantime, your chest will unclench. You'll stop being angry at the world for not "paying you back."

The world chases applause that fades by morning. We are building something in the quiet that doesn't need a single clap to stand tall.

◆◆◆

To be unusable is not to be closed.
It is to be whole.
You cannot hook what has no handle.
You cannot shake what is rooted below the noise.

YOUR BODY IS YOUR TEMPLE

We've spent a lot of time talking about the wealth you can count. Now we have to talk about the wealth you are.

The ancient Tamizh called it "Nalam". It is usually translated as health, but that is too clinical. It is better understood as wholeness. It is the realization that your body is not a tool you use. It is the ground you stand on.

Most of us treat our bodies like a rental car we plan to trash before the contract is up. We push the engine, skip the oil changes, and wonder why the dashboard is lighting up with warning signs in our thirties and early forties. But here's the cold truth: there is no "return" desk. This is the only vehicle you get. If the hardware fails, the software—your wisdom, your love, your purpose—has nowhere to run.

The Debt We Don't Discuss

In your twenties, you can live on coffee, stress, and four hours of sleep. Your body is a forgiving lender. But in your thirties and beyond, the interest rates start to climb.

I have seen men spend fifteen years grinding, building businesses, chasing promotions, and sacrificing sleep, only to reach the finish line with a full bank account and a body that cannot enjoy a single cent of it. They have wealth, but no vitality, and a body that is already broken.

When you neglect your health, you aren't "saving time." You are borrowing time from your future self at a predatory interest rate. You're trading your 60s and 70s for a few extra hours of "productivity" in your 30s. That's a bad deal.

Strength is Just "Useful Capacity"

We have been lied to about strength. The social mirror tells you that strength is about having a certain look, broad shoulders for photos and a low body fat percentage for the ego. That is vanity, and vanity is exhausting.

It's the ability to carry your kid for three miles when they get tired without your knees screaming. It's the ability to help a friend move a couch without throwing your back out for a week. It's the stamina to stay sharp at a 4:00 PM meeting when everyone else is crashing on caffeine.

Comfort is a slow poison. It dulls your blade. Friction is what sharpens you. Lifting something heavy, walking farther than you want to, and sweating when it is inconvenient all serve a purpose.

Stop training for the mirror. Start training for the mission. Ask yourself, *"Am I physically capable of being the man my family and my work require me to be?"* If you are winded walking up two flights of stairs, you are not "strong." You are an asset that is depreciating.

The Internal Noise (The Steady Mind)

If your body is the hardware, your mind is the operating system. Right now, most of us have too many tabs open. We are living in a "Reactive Storm." We wake up to notifications, work through emails, and go to sleep scrolling through other people's highlight reels.

We call it "stress," but really, it's just Clutter.

A "Steady Mind" isn't about being a monk on a mountain. It's about Discernment. It's the ability to sit in a room and know which voice is yours and which voice is just the "Thinking Mirror" trying to scare you.

When you don't tend to this inner quiet, you don't make decisions—you just have reactions. You snap at your kids because you're "tired." You make bad business moves because you're "anxious." That's not a man in control; that's a man whose hardware is overheating.

The Choice: Comfort or Consequence

You cannot have a life of perpetual ease and a life of real power. They don't live in the same house.

Every time you choose the couch over the walk, or the processed sugar over the real meal, you are making a trade. You are trading Future Agency for Current Comfort.

The ease we chase, the extra drink, the late-night doomscrolling, the skipped workout, comes with a heavy tax. It shows up years later as a body that cannot move and a mind that cannot focus. A life of consequence means accepting a small amount of voluntary hardship today so you are not forced into involuntary suffering tomorrow.

The Daily Maintenance

Don't do this out of guilt. Guilt is a weak fuel; it burns out in a week. Do it because you want the Agency to live a full life.

1. Move for Utility

Don't just "exercise." Train your body to be a tool. Push, pull, carry, and squat. If you can't move your own body weight comfortably, you are a prisoner in your own skin. Find a way to get your heart rate up until you're breathing hard at least three times a week. It's a bribe for your sanity.

2. Clean the Fuel

You wouldn't put cheap, watered-down gas in a high-performance engine. Stop doing it to yourself. If it comes in a crinkly plastic bag with a shelf life of three years, it's not fuel—it's a distraction. Eat things that lived, grew, or ran. Protein isn't just for bodybuilders; it's the bricks and mortar of your entire system.

3. Protect the "Repair Shift" (Sleep)

Sleep isn't for the lazy; it's for the elite. It's when your brain flushes out the toxins and your muscles rebuild. If you're cheating on sleep to get more work done, you're just making your work shittier. A man who sleeps well is a man who can think clearly under pressure.

4. The 10-Minute Silence

You don't need to be a "Zen Master." Just sit. No phone, no music, no talking. Ten minutes. Watch how fast your brain tries to run away. That "itch" to check your phone? That's the addiction. Sit through it. That's how you get the steering wheel back.

Why This is the "First Wealth"

You can have the wisdom of a sage and the bank account of a king, but if you're trapped in a body that's failing and a mind that's screaming, you are poor.

Body is the ultimate luxury. It's the freedom to choose your actions rather than having your limitations choose them for you.

Build your foundation. Not for the applause, but so that when life asks something of you, and it will, you can look it in the eye and say, *"I'm ready. I was built for this."*

◆◆◆

Don't just live in your body.
Inhabit it.
It is the only home your soul will know.

THE INVISIBLE CURRICULUM

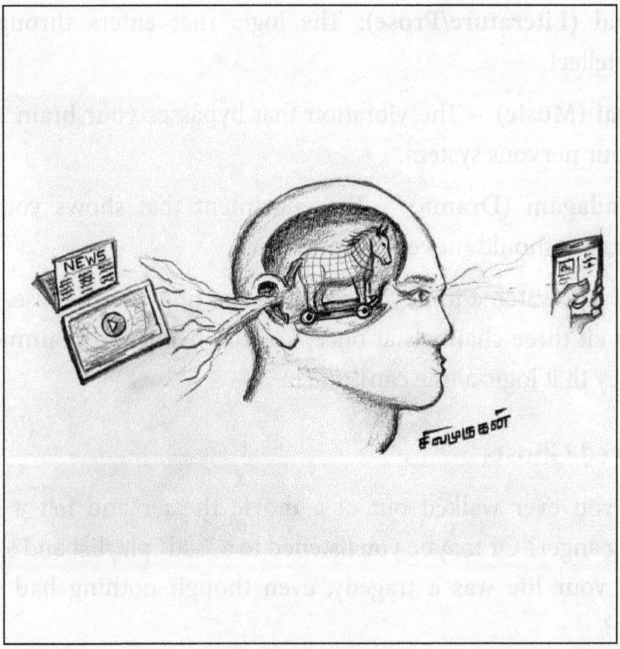

We love to tell ourselves that movies, music, and the endless scroll of social media are "just entertainment." We say we're just "switching off" our brains after a long day. We sit back, we laugh, we cry, and we think we move on.

That is the most dangerous lie we tell ourselves.

Stories are never empty. They are delivery systems. They are the Trojan Horses of the modern world. You think you're just watching a three-hour action flick or listening to a catchy song, but inside that "entertainment" is a cargo of assumptions, habits, and small permissions that slip into your mind while your guard is down.

In Tamizh culture, we've always understood that communication is a total takeover of the human system. We call it **Muthamizh**—the three living vessels:

1. **Iyal (Literature/Prose)**: The logic that enters through your intellect.
2. **Isai (Music)** – The vibration that bypasses your brain and hits your nervous system.
3. **Nadagam (Drama)** – The enactment that shows you how a person should move, talk, and react.

When you watch a film, you aren't just getting one of these. You are opening all three channels at once. You are being "programmed" at a frequency that logic alone can't touch.

Borrowed Ghosts

Have you ever walked out of a movie theater and felt a strange, lingering anger? Or maybe you listened to a "sad" playlist and suddenly felt like your life was a tragedy, even though nothing had actually changed?

When I was younger, I watched a lot of those films where the "cool" hero was always a loner who distrusted everyone. I didn't have any reason to distrust my friends, but a habit started to form. I started looking for "the angle." I watched movies where partners betrayed each other for a plot twist, and suddenly, a small, useless doubt started living in my house. I might look at my partner and think, *"What if she does that to me?"*

Those doubts didn't come from my life. I didn't earn them. **I borrowed them from a script written by someone** I've never met, who was likely just trying to sell tickets.

This is how society's "Normal" changes. First, it's a story on a screen. Then, it's an act in a scene. Finally, it's a habit in your living room. If every "strong man" on screen is a womanizer or a drunk, your brain starts to believe that those are the "tools" of masculinity.

The Attention Trade

The entertainment business is a multi-billion dollar machine, and its fuel is your **attention**. It doesn't care if a story leaves you feeling peaceful, steady, or wise. In fact, peace is boring to a scriptwriter. Confusion, rage, and scandal sell better.

The people making this stuff aren't your mentors. They aren't checking to see if their "content" helps you keep a Steady Mind or True Friendship. They are trading on your emotions to keep you watching. They will glamorize infidelity as "passion" and dress up greed as "ambition" because it makes for a "hookier" trailer.

This isn't an argument to go live in a cave and throw away your TV. It's an argument for Consciousness. It's about realizing that every time you hit "Play," you are having a conversation with the creator of that work. You need to be a very picky conversationalist.

The Media Audit: Cleaning the Filter

If you ate junk food for every meal, you'd expect your body to fall apart. Why do we expect our minds to stay healthy on a diet of digital trash?

If you want to reclaim your mind, you have to start with ruthless attention.

1. The Post-Game Analysis Don't just turn off the TV and go to bed. Take ten seconds to check your "internal weather." After a show or a scroll session, ask:

- *"Do I feel lighter or duller?"*
- *"Do I feel braver, or am I suddenly more suspicious of my neighbors?"*

- *"Does this story make me want to open my hand or clench my fist?"*

2. **Choosing Your Teachers** Think of the 16 Wealths. Does the media you consume nourish them?

- *Does it model Truthfulness, or does it make lying look like a "smart" move?*
- *Does it encourage A Loving Partner, or does it make commitment look like a prison sentence? If the story is consistently attacking your wealth, stop letting it into your house. Unfollow the accounts that stir up vanity. Delete the songs that make you feel like a victim.*

3. **The Ritual of the "Deep Buy-In"** When an ad or a trend tells you that you need a certain "thing" to be happy, slow down. Ask: "Who wrote this script? And what do they gain if I believe I'm not enough without this purchase?" Usually, the answer is "Money," and the person losing is you.

You Are the Medium

Finally, remember that you aren't just a consumer; you are a creator.

The stories you tell your friends, the way you speak about your wife, and the "jokes" you share are your own drama. You are enacting a script for your children and your peers. If you allow careless, toxic stories to shape you, you will pass that poison on to the people who trust you.

Be the filter. Be the man who chooses his "ghosts" carefully. This book you're reading right now? It's a medium, too. I'm giving you these ideas on purpose. But don't just "accept" them. Test them. See if they make your life feel more solid or more hollow.

Choose your stories with the same gravity you would use to choose a doctor for your child. Guard your attention. It is the only thing you truly own. Let in what lifts you, what steadies you, and what teaches you to be the man you intended to be. Let the rest pass by like wind through a screen door.

◆ ◆ ◆

What you watch, you practice.
What you hear, you hum.
What you read, you become.

HOW SHAME BECOMES A CURRENCY

You're sitting in the breakroom, or maybe a café. You open your lunch, a simple bowl of millet, some greens, maybe a bit of homemade pickle. The smell is familiar; it's the smell of home, of your grandmother's kitchen, of the earth.

Then, a colleague walks by. He's holding a branded bag of fast food or a sleek, overpriced wrap. He looks at your bowl, smirks, and says, "Still eating that 'farmer food,' man? When are you going to join the 21st century?"

A heat rises in your ears. Your throat tightens. In that split second, you don't see a nutritious meal that keeps you lean and strong. You see "poverty." You see "backwardness." You feel an urge to close the lid, to laugh it off, or to explain that you're just "trying a new diet."

Why? Why does a comment from a guy who is likely one medical bill away from bankruptcy make you feel small?

That heat isn't just an emotion. It's the sound of a trap snapping shut. It's the signal that you've handed over your "Steady Mind" and your "Good Name" to be judged by someone who doesn't even know who they are.

The Loss of Our Bond with Earth and Community

To understand the heat that rises in your cheeks, we have to look at how our sense of belonging was deliberately reshaped.

For thousands of years in Tamizh Nadu, our homes were built to breathe. At the front stood the Thinnai, a raised earthen porch that served as more than architecture. It was a way of life. It was where rain was watched, travelers were welcomed, and elders kept a steady mind by remaining connected to the street. A home did not end at the front door. It flowed naturally into the community.

Then came the architects of status. They did not arrive with force. They arrived with a new definition of privacy.

They brought high compound walls, tinted glass, and sealed, air-conditioned boxes that cut us off from the wind and from one another. They labeled the Thinnai as primitive and village-style. They taught us that openness was vulnerability and that retreating behind gates, cameras, and guards was success.

What they changed was not just the floor plan. They altered our internal mirror.

We were taught to look at openness and see backwardness. Hospitality became something to hide. Our closeness to the earth was rebranded as dustiness. Slowly, we accepted the lie. We traded the cool, breezy wisdom of the porch for the expensive isolation of the luxury apartment, all to avoid being judged by those who mistake a cage for a castle.

And so we lost something quietly. The threshold, once a living space between self and society, became a line of defense. Where connection once lived, suspicion moved in. Where belonging once flowed, silence settled.

When we abandon small, human spaces, we lose more than architecture. We lose daily practices of humility, generosity, and presence. We lose the places where character was shaped without effort.

This is how a spatial betrayal becomes a personal one. Change itself is not the problem, because change is inevitable. **The problem arises when change is accepted without awareness. If you consciously choose a different way of living, that choice is valid. But if you were taught to feel ashamed of what once worked simply because someone needed to sell a new idea, then the choice was never truly yours.** We do not have to remain in the same place forever, but we should understand why we are leaving and what we are sacrificing when we do. Without that clarity, movement becomes confusion, and isolation is mistaken for progress.

The Modern Shame Machine

Today, corporations with marketing budgets larger than the GDP of small nations. Their entire business model is based on creating a void in your chest and then selling you a "bridge" to cross it.

Think about how they work. To sell you a new car, they don't talk about the engine. They talk about "status." They imply that if you drive your current car, you are stagnant. They create a "Social Mirror" that reflects a version of you that is "less than" until you make the purchase.

- **The Clothing Trap:** They mock your comfortable, local cottons as "unprofessional" or "boring" so they can sell you a brand-name suit that makes you sweat and costs two months' salary.

- **The Tech Trap:** They make you feel "left behind" because your phone doesn't have three cameras, as if the quality of your photos determines the quality of your life.
- **The Lifestyle Trap:** They show you images of "success" that always involve spending, expensive items, foreign vacations, luxury watches. They never show you "success" as a man who is debt-free, healthy, and sleeping peacefully next to a partner who actually respects him for who he is, not what he wears.

They make you uncomfortable in your own skin because a comfortable man is un-marketable. A man who knows he is "enough" is a nightmare for a consumer economy.

The Fragility of the "Cool"

Look closely at the people who mock you. Look at the "colleague" with the fast food and the expensive items.

Is he a pillar of strength? Or is he a man who is terrified of being "found out"? Most people who mock the "native," the "simple," or the "authentic" are the most fragile of all. They are performing for a mirror that is never satisfied. Their "Wealth" is often just debt dressed up in a logo.

A truly powerful man doesn't need you to feel small. A man who is rooted in the Sixteen Wealths doesn't care if his shoes are the "right" brand or if his lunch looks "modern." He knows that Wholeness beats "Status" every single day. He has a Steady Mind, so the "Thinking Mirror" can't rattle him with a joke about millet.

The Way Back: The Work of Unshaming

The way out of this trap isn't to get angry at the world. It's to become Conscious. When you feel that heat in your cheeks, that's your cue to start digging.

1. **Trace the Hook** When you feel ashamed of your car, your clothes, or your "farmer food," stop. Ask: *"Who taught me this*

was shameful? What are they trying to sell me as the cure?" If the answer involves you spending money or changing your values to feel "accepted," you are being manipulated. Name it. Say to yourself, *"This shame isn't mine. It's a commercial I've been forced to watch."*

2. **The "Solitude Test"** Ask yourself: *"If I were the last man on Earth, would I still want this 'expensive' thing?* If the answer is No, then your shame is just a performance for people who don't actually matter to your long-term wealth.

3. **Own the "Backwardness"** If someone calls you "old-fashioned" or "backwards" for honoring your roots, living simply, or refusing to chase trends, smile. Say, *"Yeah, it works for me."* There is nothing more terrifying to a manipulator than a man who cannot be shamed. When you own the thing they are trying to use against you, their power evaporates instantly.

Walking on Your Own Soil

You are not poor because you want less. You are not "behind" because you value the ancient over the trendy.

Think of a **Neem tree.** It is bitter. It doesn't try to be a sweet mango. It doesn't apologize for its bitterness. And because of that bitterness, it is one of the most powerful medicines on Earth. It is unapologetically itself. It doesn't check with the other trees to see if its leaves are the right shade of green.

You have a choice. You can spend your life trying to polish a "Social Mirror" that will never reflect anything but your own anxiety. Or you can step off the board and start building the **Solid Floor** we talked about.

Eat your "farmer food" with pride. Wear your clothes for comfort and character. Speak your truth without checking the room for approval.

The game of shame only works if you agree to look into their mirror. Put it down. Look at the earth under your feet. You are already standing on everything you need. You are not a "consumer" in a market; you are a man in a lineage. Start acting like it.

◆◆◆

Don't wear their uniform.
Wear your skin.
It fits you perfectly.

THE MODERN INDENTURE

On Debt & Freedom

We like to tell ourselves we're free. We have the fancy job titles, the credit cards with the "Elite" branding, and the keys to a house in a good neighborhood. But beneath the polite language of "asset building" and "low-interest EMIs," a quiet, brutal bargain is being made: you are trading the pulse of your future for the polish of your present.

In ancient times, if a man took money he couldn't pay back, he became an indentured servant. He worked the master's fields until the debt was cleared. He didn't own his time; he didn't own his labor.

Today, we don't use iron chains; we use digital signatures. The shape of the life remains the same: you have handed over your future years—the years you haven't even lived yet—to a bank in exchange for a thing you probably didn't need.

Think about that subtle, cold shiver that hits you when you see a neighbor's new SUV and think, "I earn enough, I can handle that monthly payment." That sentence is the sound of a trap snapping shut. The moment you sign for a car, a house, or a lifestyle you can't actually afford, you aren't just buying a thing. You are buying a **mandatory obligation** to stay exactly where you are. You have just sold your right to take a risk, to change your mind, or to tell a bad boss to shove it.

The Weight of the 1st

There is a specific kind of exhaustion that comes with debt. It is not the good kind of tired you feel after a day of honest work. It is a **hollow, grinding fatigue.** It is the feeling of waking up on the first of the month and realizing that your salary, the money you traded thirty days of your life for, is already gone before it even reaches your account.

It's already been promised to the car company, the home loan provider, and the credit card bank. You aren't working for yourself. You aren't working for your family. You are working for them. When you are deep in the "Chain," you become a man who is "For Sale." You become "manageable." You stay in the toxic job because you have to. You swallow the disrespect because you have to. You stop being a man of **Conscious Strength** and become a man of **Necessary Compliance**. That is the emotional tax of debt: it robs you of your backbone.

The Two Weights: The Chain vs. The Tool

We have to be honest here. Not all borrowing is a crime against your future. But as a man looking to build the Sixteen Wealths, you must know what you are putting around your neck.

- **The Chain (Consumer Debt)** This is money borrowed to buy things that rot or lose value. The "lifestyle" car. The "luxury" wedding. The "status" watch. This kind of debt is a chain because it produces nothing but stress. It demands your future hours, the hours you should be spending watching your children grow or building your own dream, and hands them to a billionaire's balance sheet. It turns your time into a monthly payment for an image that is already fading.
- **The Tool (Leverage)** This is borrowing to expand your capacity. It's a calculated risk to build a business, to learn a high-value skill, or to secure a modest home that serves as a fortress for your family.

The difference is simple: A **Tool** eventually sets you free. A Chain keeps you in your place. A sovereign man respects the power of a tool, but he fears the "comfort" of the cage.

The Psychology of Public Begging

Why do we do it? Why do we sign away our freedom for leather seats and a logo?

Let's be honest: **It's a form of begging.** When you buy a house you can't afford and think, "Now people will respect me," you are begging for validation. You are trading your independence for applause from people who aren't even looking at you, they're too busy worrying about their own debts.

We call it "smart finance," but a better name is Impatient Finance. We lack the patience to build slowly, to save, and to earn our status. So we mortgage our 50s so we can look "successful" in our 30s. We trade A Steady Mind for a shiny driveway. It's a hollow, heartbreaking trade.

The 5 Moves to Reclaim Your Sovereignty

If you want to be a man who cannot be used, you have to stop the bleeding. Here is how you start building a floor instead of a cage.

- **Name the Slavery:** Before you take a loan, write down what you are sacrificing. Write: "*To have this car, I am giving up my freedom to quit this job for the next seven years.*" See the invisible price tag.

- **Redefine Respect:** Real respect isn't built on things that can be repossessed. Real respect comes from **Capability** and **The Power** to Walk Away. The tiger in the zoo looks impressive, but he's still behind bars. The tiger in the wild owns his time.

- **The "Runway" Metric:** Ask yourself: *How many months could my family survive if I stopped working today? If the answer is less than six months, you aren't "successful"*—you are indentured. Your first priority isn't a "new lifestyle"; it's building that six-month fortress of cash.

- **Practice Delayed Possession:** Pick one thing you were going to buy on credit. Stop. Save for it. Wait until you can buy it in full. The waiting will teach you more than the owning ever will.
- **The Sovereignty Question:** Before every signature, ask: "*Does this debt work for me, or do I work for the debt?*"

The Tale of Two Lives

Imagine two men who want the same SUV.

The first man saves for three years. He buys a used model in cash. He owns the car. If he wants to take a three-month break to learn a new language or start a side business, he can. His map of choices is huge.

The second man signs a 7-year EMI for the latest model. He drives it home today. He looks "better" for about a week. But now, his map has shrunk. He must earn a specific amount every month. He can't take risks. He can't speak up at work. He has an appointment with the bank every month, and that appointment is non-negotiable.

Years later, the first man has **Options**. The second man has **Obligations**.

The Final Measure: The Power of the Exit

We have been taught that wealth is the sum of what you can gather. I am telling you that wealth is the sum of what you can **leave behind.**

True net worth isn't found on a bank statement or a car registration. It is found in the answer to one question: "How much of my soul do I have to sell every morning to keep this lifestyle running?"

If you are staying in a job that kills your spirit, working for a man you don't respect, or compromising your Truthfulness just to pay for a house you only use to sleep in, then you don't own that house. That house owns you. It is a parasite disguised as an achievement.

The Most Expensive Word in the World

The most powerful word a man can own is **"No."**

But "No" has a price. To say "No" to a paycheck, you need a Steady Mind and a literal floor of savings. If you are drowning in debt, your "No" is weak. It's a whisper. But when you own your life, when you have traded your impatience for your possibility, your "No" becomes a fortress.

The freedom to walk away from a life you hate is worth more than every luxury item ever manufactured. Buy only what you can truly own. If a possession requires you to pawn your peace of mind, your time, or your courage just to keep it—it is too expensive. You are paying for it with the only currency that matters: **your limited days on this earth.**

True wealth is the state of having a Zero Balance in the ledgers of others. Whether it is a high-interest EMI for a car you don't need, or a decades old Nandrikadan (debt of gratitude) that keeps you from speaking your truth, any debt that restricts your "Power to Walk Away" is a threat to your sovereignty.

The goal of a man of Conscious Strength is to move from Obligation to Contribution. You don't work because you have to pay the bank; you work because you choose to build. You don't serve your family because you owe them your life; you serve them because you love them with your freedom.

The goal isn't to look wealthy. The goal is to be unshakable.

◆◆◆

Your wealth is not what you show.
It is what you can walk away from.
Freedom is measured in exits, not entrances.

THE THIEF OF TIME

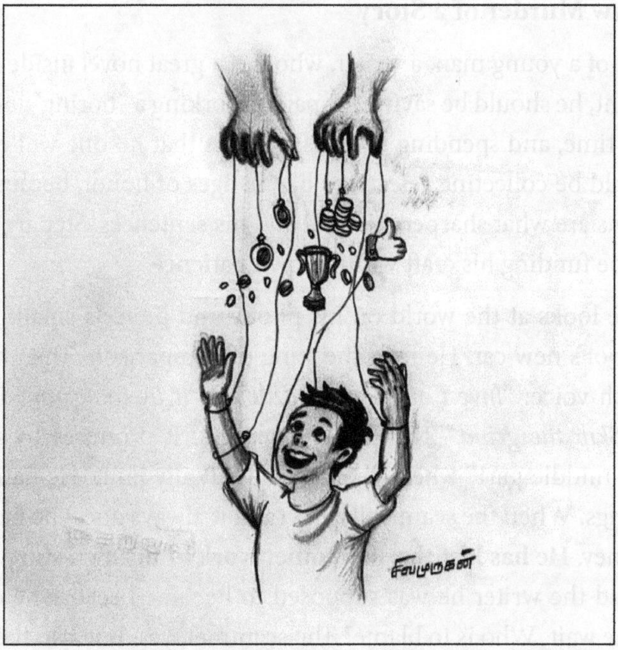

We see it every day, the headlines about scams, the local betrayals, the cousins who lost everything in a "double-your-money" scheme, and the men who end up behind bars for a quick grab. We shake our heads and offer the usual reasons: *"He had a hard childhood." "The economy is a mess." "Society failed him."*

Those reasons are true enough. Life can be brutal. But as men who are hunting for clarity, we have to go a step deeper. Beyond why they did it, we must ask: **How did they justify it to themselves in the dark?** The "how" is always the same: **They wanted the fruit without planting the tree.** They wanted the harvest today, without the years of watering, the aching back from the tilling, and the long, silent months of waiting. They wanted it now. This isn't just a quirk of impulse; it is a philosophy of theft. And the person being robbed most isn't the victim. It is the man himself.

The Slow Murder of a Story

Think of a young man, a writer, who has a great novel inside him. To do it right, he should be saving for paper, working a "boring" job to buy himself time, and spending months on edits that no one will ever see. He should be collecting rejections like badges of honor, because those rejections are what sharpen his soul and his sentences. Step by step, he should be funding his craft with his own patience.

But he looks at the world on his phone and he feels small. He sees a neighbor's new car. He feels the sting of comparison. Then he hears a smooth voice: *"Invest one lakh and double it by tomorrow. Don't be a fool. Skip the grind."* The shortcut glitters. It promises to skip the "boring middle part" where character is actually built. He hands over his savings. When the scam collapses (and it always does) he hasn't just lost money. **He has lost the slow, quiet work of his own story.** He has murdered the writer he was supposed to become because he couldn't stand the wait. Who is to blame? The scammer, yes. But also the part of him that refused to be ordinary for a while.

The Theft of Self-Trust

Gambling, lotteries, "insider" tips—they all whisper the same poison: "You don't have to build. You can just win." But winning without building is a theft from your own future. A man who steals gold takes from someone else's pocket. But a man who chases instant profit robs his own time, his own learning, and his own competency.

We often call this "greed," but look closer. It is actually sadder than greed. At its root, it is a **deep, shivering distrust in your own capacity.** It is a man saying to himself: "I am not capable of growing what I need. I am not smart enough or strong enough to endure the process. My only hope is a miracle or a trick." So you trade your **Integrity** for haste. You trade your **Good Name** for a quick headline. The money you bring home tastes thin because you know exactly how it arrived. It fills the belly, but it leaves the spirit starving.

The Ache at the Edge of the Bed

There is a truth that no shortcut artist will tell you: **Whatever is built slowly, enters your hands and stays. Whatever is taken quickly, burns them.** Consider the man who brings home "quick" or stolen money to feed his family. On the surface, it looks like a win. The plate is full. The children are eating. The wife is smiling because the bills are paid. But that man sits at the edge of the bed at 2:00 AM and feels an old, thin ache.

He looks at his children's faces and thinks, "*This wasn't provided by my strength. It was provided by my fear.*" The money buys relief. The house may stand, but the pillars under it? the stories of hard work, the lessons of resilience, the calm confidence that a father's labor provides are cracking. He is a ghost in his own home, living on borrowed time and a stolen image. He is passing on a false currency to his children, teaching them that the result matters more than the human being who creates it. He is teaching them that their father is a man who can be bought.

Why the "Quick Fix" Fails the Wound

Why does quick wealth matter so much to us, even when it destroys our character? Because it promises to fix an immediate wound: hunger, the shame of being "less than," or the sharp, judgmental glance of a neighbor. Instant money offers a fast bandage for the discomfort of comparison.

But a quick fix cannot mend the deeper thing: **The need to trust yourself.** When you take the easy path, you are telling your soul that you are a "sucker" for trying to be honest. You are reinforcing the idea that the only way to "get ahead" is to cheat the system. And once you believe that, you have lost the most important wealth of all: **Wisdom.**

The Defense Against the "Now"

We have to build a fortress against the urge for the "Now." It isn't about being a saint; it's about being a builder who wants his structure to stand for a hundred years.

1. **The 5-Day Cooling Rule** When an offer arrives that smells like easy gain, your blood will heat up. That heat is your enemy. Pause. Say to yourself, "*Tell me more.*" Then, give your mind five days. Not five minutes to process it. Scams and bad decisions rely on heat and urgency. Time cools them. If it is a true opportunity, it will still be there in five days. If it is a trap, the "glitter" will fade, and you will see the hook.
2. **Name the Panic** If you are tempted to gamble, cheat, or take a shady shortcut, do not call it **"ambition."** Call it what it is: **"Panic."** Be brutally honest. Say, "*I am worried about my family's safety, and I don't trust myself to fix it slowly.*" Naming the fear takes away its mystery. It forces you to map a real path—saving a little each month, learning one skill at a time, trading the "image" of success for a plan of small, certain steps.
3. **The Legacy Test** Treat your integrity like the greatest inheritance you can leave. A man with a Good Name opens doors that money cannot buy. If you are tempted by a scheme, imagine sitting your son or daughter down in ten years. You have to tell them the story of how you got the money for their college or your house.
    - Can you tell that story with your head held high?
    - Or will you have to edit the truth? If you cannot tell the story plainly and proudly, do not take the money.

The Practicality of the Slow Build

This isn't moralizing; it is practical survival. A man who builds slowly can handle the storms. He sleeps. He teaches by example. His children learn the "craft of life." A man who takes fast will always be one gust of wind away from total ruin.

Try this: The Two-List System.

- **The Slow List:** Write five things you can do this week that build quietly. Calling a difficult client, learning a new technical skill, fixing a broken process in your business.
- **The Refusal List:** Write five "quick" offers you will refuse outright this month. The "insider" tip, the lottery ticket, the "easy" shortcut.

Carry these lists. When the instant urge comes, read them. You will be surprised how often the pause reroutes your heart.

Remember the sixteen true wealths. Money calls the loudest because it is the only one that is visible to strangers. But a life made only of things that show is brittle. Health, A Steady Mind, Truthfulness, and Friendship do not glitter in the market, but they are the anchors that hold the ship when the hurricane comes.

The Final Answer

The world will always sell shortcuts at every corner. It will mock your "slow" progress. But dignity is bought only with patience.

If you want to bring wealth to your family that they can remember without a side of shame, spend your life like a builder. Mine your own mountain. Plant your own trees. The slow things that grow are the only things you can hand down without an apology.

When the quick-money whisper returns, answer it quietly and plainly: "No. I am building."

It will cost you more. It will take you longer. It will ask for the courage to be "ordinary" while everyone else is pretending to be "extraordinary."

But in the end, you will have a kind of wealth the thief cannot touch: a life you earned, a sleep that is steady, and a name you can speak aloud in any room.

Start small. Choose one thing this month to earn rather than just acquire. Save for it. Work for it. When you finally have it in your hands, look at it. You will understand why the waiting was not a loss, but an investment in the man you have become.

Your time was not stolen.. it was sown.

◆ ◆ ◆

Want the fruit?
Plant the tree.
Or steal it
and starve while holding it.

THE TREASURY

On perspective & Corruption

You wake up, you pick up your phone, and you scroll the headlines. Within thirty seconds, that familiar heat backs up behind your eyes. You see the corruption, the blatant incompetence, the corporate greed that seems to have no bottom. It feels like the government is a circus, your manager is a parasite, and the whole system is a rigged game designed to keep you small.

It feels obvious. It feels like the "truth."

But here is a dangerous question: What if your "truth" is someone else's poison?

The Poison on the Plate

Imagine two villages. In the first, the **Jackfruit** is life. It's what fathers feed their sons to make them strong. It's a symbol of celebration and survival. In the second village, the Jackfruit is a death sentence. For generations, their bodies haven't been able to digest it. To them, it's not food; it's a slow, agonizing poison.

One day, a man from the first village meets a man from the second. With a heart full of genuine kindness, he offers a ripe piece of fruit.

"Eat," he says. *"This will make you powerful."* The other man doesn't see a gift. He sees an assassin. He recoils. He shouts. Accusations start flying. The argument becomes a fight, and the fight becomes a story that both tribes will tell for a hundred years to justify hating the other.

Both men are "right." Both are also dangerously wrong because they assume their reality is the only one.

We do this every single day. We judge a person's politics, their religion, or their "lazy" work habits without knowing the "digestive system" that shaped them. We condemn a man for being suspicious without realizing he grew up in a house where trust was a liability. We call someone "ignorant" because they don't value what we value, never stopping to ask: **"What if, in his world, my 'medicine' feels like death?"**

The Treasury Test

It's easy to hate a corrupt politician on a screen. It's a low-cost hobby. But let's bring the mirror closer.

Imagine it's 2:00 AM. You are handed a key to the national treasury. There are no cameras. There is no audit trail. No one will ever know. And right now, your life is falling apart. Your daughter needs a surgery you can't afford. Your parents are living under a roof that's about to collapse. That key can solve every single problem your family has tonight.

What does your hand do?

Let's be real, man to man. Is your hand perfectly steady? Or is there a moment where the "right" thing starts to blur with the "necessary" thing?

The man who takes a million-dollar bribe didn't start there. He started ten years ago by keeping the extra change at the grocery store. He started by exaggerating a travel expense. He started with the "harmless" lie on an invoice. Corruption isn't a monster that falls from the sky; it's a long, slow habit of tiny untruths.

We point at the "sin" on the news because it makes us feel like we are a different species. We aren't. We are just versions of the same choice. If you can't be trusted with the "small" change, you have no right to be surprised when the man with the "big" key fails his test, too.

The River and the Bed

Society is a mirror. It is the sum of millions of private, lonely choices. If the reflection looks ugly, we can't just blame the person who held the mirror. We have to look at the habits we've allowed to rot the image.

Think of it this way: **If you want to change the river, you have to change the bed.**

You can curse the current all you want. You can scream at the water for being muddy. But the water will always flow where the shape of the ground allows it to flow. Our "bed" is our silent permissions—the shortcuts we justify, the lies we tell to "protect" ourselves, the moments we choose comfort over **Justice.**

The Work of the Quiet Revolution

If you want to stop the rot, you don't start with a protest. You start with your own "bed."

1. **Drop the Ideology:** Before you call a neighbor evil or a colleague a fool, stop. Ask: "*What Jackfruit am I offering that feels like poison to them?*" Understanding isn't the same as agreeing. It's just the process of mapping the world so you don't keep running into walls.
2. **The Cashier Test:** The revolution against corruption starts when you return the extra ten dollars the tired cashier gave you by mistake. It starts when you refuse to take credit for a teammate's idea, even if it would get you a promotion. It starts in the places where **no one will ever applaud you.** That is the only place where true **Truthfulness** is built.

3. **The Blueprint of Repair:** Look at the sixteen wealths. They aren't just for you. They are the bricks for a better city. When you build a Steady Mind, you become the calm center in a panicked town.

The "Sucker" Barrier

The hardest part of this is not the honesty itself. It is the feeling that you are a fool for even trying. You will see men who have lied, cheated, and stepped on others to reach the top. They have the bigger house, the louder laugh, and the seat at the head of the table. Your thinking mirror will look at them and then look at you, returning extra change or staying late to fix a mistake no one saw, and it will whisper, *"You're a sucker. The game is rigged, and you're the only one still following the rules."*

That whisper is the ultimate test of a man's strength. Remember this. The man who cheats to win is always a tenant in his own life. He owes his success to the lie. The moment that lie is exposed, his world collapses. When you build on truth, you own the ground you stand on. You are not being "nice." You are becoming something else entirely. You are building a form of success that does not require permission and cannot be taken away by a whistleblower, an audit, or the shifting moods of the crowd.

One Honest Choice

You won't fix the government by yourself this week. You won't end corporate greed by tomorrow. But you can stop feeding the "bed" that makes the river run the way it does.

Imagine a world where every man decided to be "ordinary" enough to be honest. It wouldn't make the news. It would be tedious, quiet, repetitive work. But after a generation of men who refused to tell the "easy" lie, the bed would shift. The current would change. The river that our children have to swim in would finally be clear.

We are all villagers. we are all offering our version of the "Jackfruit" and calling it the absolute truth.

Wisdom doesn't live in the shouting. It lives in the patient learning of another man's map. Build the world you want the same way you build a muscle: one honest choice at a time. One honest life.

The soil changes, and the future grows quietly from the earth you Tilled today.

◆ ◆ ◆

A steady mind in a noisy town
is a revolution.
A truthful man in a corrupt system
is a seed of a new world.

I AM THE STRONGEST MAN EVER

Strength. It is the one word every man wants carved onto his headstone, yet it is the one word we understand the least.

If you ask the average guy on the street what strength is, he'll point to the man with the loudest voice, the biggest bank account, or the most "hustle." We've been conditioned to believe that strength is the ability to bend the world to your will. We think it's about making people do what you want—whether you buy their loyalty, threaten their security, or manipulate their emotions. We see a man who "crushes" his rivals and we call him a titan.

But look at that man's eyes when the cameras are off. That isn't strength. That is Force. And **force is almost always just fear wearing a very expensive costume.**

Real strength is something much quieter, much heavier, and infinitely harder to find. It is the power to do what your heart knows is right, even when the entire world is screaming at you to do the opposite. It is the ability to be the only person in the room who doesn't fold.

The Silent Tests

We think strength is found on a battlefield or in a boardroom, but those are just the stages. The actual strength happens in the "private minutes" where no one is watching.

Let's be honest about your life for a second.

You are sitting in a meeting. Your manager is spouting some absolute bullshit, presenting a lie as a fact to save his own skin. You know the truth. Your palms are sweaty. Your heart is hammering against your ribs like a trapped bird. Do you speak? Or does the fear of losing your "status" or your paycheck tie your tongue in a knot?

Or think about the person you love. Maybe they come from the "wrong" background, the "wrong" community, or speak the "wrong" language according to your social circle. Do you stand by that love? Or do you tear your own heart out and walk away because you can't handle the whispers of people whose opinions you don't even respect?

We see corruption in our local councils, our companies, and our friendship groups. We see the "small" cheat, the "minor" betrayal. Do you call it out? Or do you look at the floor and tell yourself, *"It's not my fight,"* while a piece of your soul quietly dies?

In a thousand tiny, silent moments, we are given a choice: Do I want the **Reality** of strength, or the **Performance** of it? Most of us choose the performance. We mistake being "rigid" for being "brave." We mistake being "loud" for being "powerful."

The Cage of the "Powerful"

We are told to envy the politician who commands crowds or the businessman who dominates industries. But I want you to look closer at the "titan."

The politician isn't a leader; he is a hostage. He is a slave to the next poll, terrified of a single rumor, and constantly performing for an invisible audience that could turn on him in a heartbeat. He doesn't own his voice. The "successful" businessman who crushes his rivals is often a man chained to his next quarterly report, his peace of mind mortgaged to a market he can't control. He can't sleep without a pill, and he can't be honest without a lawyer.

Are these men strong? Or are they just living in the most decorated cages on earth?

You aren't seeing their power. You are seeing your own projection of what you think power looks like. You see the crown, but you don't see the neck-ache that comes from wearing it. You see the costume; you don't see the cage.

The Invisible Spine

Real strength is invisible. It doesn't need a microphone or a trophy. It is the man who says "No" when everyone else is nodding like a toy. It is the man who walks away from a dishonest profit, even when he knows he could have gotten away with it. It is the father who stays gentle and present with his children after a day that would have broken a lesser man.

This kind of strength doesn't come from your triceps or your wallet. It comes from Truthfulness that you have practiced until it has become your literal spine.

In the ancient Tamizh list of the sixteen wealths, Strength isn't a standalone item. It is the **Protector**.

- Without it, your **Money** just makes you a target for every shark in the water.
- Without it, your **Good Name** is just a fragile mask that a single lie can shatter.
- Without it, your **Friendships** are just transactions that end when the money runs out.
- Without it, **Justice** is just a word you use when it's convenient.

The strongest man on this planet is not the one who controls a million people. He is the man who has finally mastered himself.

The Internal Battlefield

Your real battle isn't out there. It's in the space between your ears. It's the gap between knowing what is right and finding the raw, bleeding courage to actually do it.

So, ask yourself the hard question: **Do you want to look strong, or do you want to be strong?**

The path to looking strong is crowded. It's loud, it's flashy, and it's paved with the approval of strangers who don't care about you. The path to being strong is solitary. It is paved with your own integrity, and the only person who will ever truly know you succeeded is you.

Strength and A Steady Mind sit beside each other for a reason. They are the guardian and the guarded. Your strength is what protects your peace from being stolen by the world. Your peace is what gives your strength the fuel to keep standing when everyone else has fallen. Without a steady mind, your strength is just "brittle aggression"—you're just a bully waiting to be broken. Without strength, your "steady mind" is just "passive avoidance"—you're just a coward pretending to be peaceful.

True strength is not a weapon you swing at the world to get your way. It is the integrity that turns you toward the truth, and the iron-willed courage that holds you there when the wind starts to howl.

Do you want to be the strongest man you've ever known? Then stop trying to move the world. Stop trying to "crush" the competition. Start by moving yourself. Start by crushing your own excuses.

The world doesn't need more men of force. It needs men of Strength. Men who own their own "Yes" and their own "No." Men who are, quite literally, "Unfit for Sale."

Start there. Move yourself. The rest is just noise.

◆ ◆ ◆

YOUR MANGO IS NOT MY NEEM

I have never seen a neem tree try to grow a mango. It sounds like a joke, doesn't it? But if you pause and really look at the biology of it, it's a profound lesson in survival. A neem tree has bitter leaves—it's built to heal, to cleanse, to endure the harshest sun. A mango tree has sweet, heavy fruit—it's built to nourish, to delight, to provide a sugary reward. They often grow just a few yards apart, drinking the same groundwater, feeling the exact same sun on their bark.

If trees had human minds, this would be a total psychological disaster.

The neem would look across the fence and think: "Everyone loves the mango. Look at the children laughing as they pick its fruit. I'm just bitter. People squint when they taste my leaves. I must become sweet. My bitterness is a failure of character."

The mango would look back and think: "I should have been a neem. The neem heals the sick. It's used in medicine. It's essential. I just feed people sugar, I'm shallow, I'm a luxury, I'm useless in a crisis."

They would spend their lives twisting their roots in an agony of anxiety. They would try to trade bark and graft branches that don't belong to them. They would die exhausted, failing to be either, and never realizing they were both exactly what the earth needed.

But nature doesn't do this. A river doesn't try to be a mountain. Fire never apologizes for not being water. Only humans do this. Only we have the unique, heartbreaking ability to sit in a forest of our own potential and wish we were a different kind of tree.

The Uniformity Trap

We boast about our "higher consciousness" and our "six senses." Yet, in this one specific way, we live far below the level of a single-sense plant. A tree never abandons its nature to please a crowd. We do it every single morning.

We wake up, look at the world, and suddenly feel "less." We see a neighbor's bigger house and our own feels like a cell. We see a friend's promotion on a screen and our quiet, steady job feels like a dead end. A question starts to rot in the back of our minds: *"Why is my world so imperfect?"*

The answer seems obvious: *"I must earn more. I must be more. I must look like them. Then I'll finally be happy."*

We've thought this way since we were kids sitting in a classroom, and it feels like basic survival. But let's be blunt: most of us aren't living so much as we are just trying to feel safe. When we don't know if we're on the right path, we look to the man next to us for proof. If he's doing the same thing, we breathe a sigh of relief. *"Good, I'm correct. I'm safe."* If he's different, we panic. We want the comfort of the crowd; sameness feels like safety. So, slowly, we all begin to march the same way—like a uniform army keeping in step, terrified to break rank, even though the path leads toward an empty cliff.

The Soul-Ache of the Pretender

The man in the small house thinks: "If I had his mansion, I'd be at peace." The man in the mansion looks out his window at the man in the small house and thinks: "He has a loving family and a quiet mind—things my debt and my lawsuits didn't buy."

In school, we long for the freedom of college. In college, we miss the simplicity of school. We hold a perfectly good apple in our hand and we can't even taste it because we're too busy longing for a banana. We discard our own leaves because we're too busy measuring them against someone else's fruit.

What are we lacking? **Respect for our own soil.**

The practice of a "whole man" isn't to collect more things, but to finally see what is already sitting in your hand. It's about knowing your own season and your own purpose—not because a billboard told you, but because you took the time to listen to your own sap flowing.

It begins with a radical, gut-level shift. Before asking **"What do they have?", you must ask "What have I been given?" Before asking "What should I become?", you must ask "What am I already?"**

Your mango is not my neem. Your river is not my mountain. And that isn't a flaw in the design—it is the point of the design.

The Display vs. The Root

Look at the sixteen wealths (Pathinaru Peru) again. Why do we crave **Money** more than the other fifteen?

It sits on display in your driveway and on your wrist. So men chase what the crowd can see and they completely forget the quiet riches that actually keep a life from collapsing: Health, Wisdom, Truthfulness. We choose what can be applauded and ignore what can be felt.

To stop comparing, you have to start **seeing**. Not measuring, but witnessing. Your worth isn't held in the other tree's branches. It's rooted in your own soil.

The Practice of Presence

Don't let this be another "nice idea." Try this tonight when the world is quiet:

Make a list of five things you already hold that money cannot buy. Be specific. Don't just write "family." Write: *"The way my daughter's hand feels in mine,"* or *"The smell of the first rain on the dry earth,"* or *"The fact that I can still walk five miles without my body failing me."*

Put that list somewhere you will see it. When the "Thinking Mirror" starts its whispering—*"Look at them, they have more"*—look at your list instead.

A life built by sight alone will always feel thin and hollow. A life rooted in your own soil grows differently. It isn't "less," and it isn't "smaller." It is simply yours.

Choose your soil. Tend it. Eat your own fruit. Let the neem be neem and the mango be mango. If you are a man who wants the sixteen wealths, you have to decide: will you live for the applause of people you don't even like, or will you finally wake up to the riches you already hold and start stewarding them well?

The reward is a kind of peace that no comparison can touch.

We don't lack what others have.
We lack respect for our own soil.
Tend your roots before you envy another's fruit.

THE RIVER AND THE POND

On sadness & expectation

Out of all the forms of wealth we've walked through so far, this one is the outlier. It's the hardest to pin down because it isn't something you can point to in your driveway or see in your reflection. It isn't an object to be possessed; it's a state of being you have to inhabit.

The ancient Tamizh wisdom called it **A Life Without Suffering.**

Now, don't let that name fool you. It sounds like a fairy tale, right? We live in a world of taxes, breakups, back pain, and grief. This wealth doesn't promise you a life where bad things don't happen. It promises a life where the pain doesn't stick. It's the difference between a wound that heals and a wound that rots.

Let's get honest about why we hurt: **Sadness is almost always the gap between how the world is and how you think it should be.** We spend our lives building these fragile "fences" of expectation. We decide how our boss should act, how our kids should speak, and how the economy should move. Then, when life which is basically just a series of unpredicted storms blows through those fences, we act shocked. We feel personally attacked. But the problem isn't the wind. **The problem is that you thought you could build a fence against the wind in the first place.**

The Pond vs. The River

I want you to really visualize two different ways of being a man.

Imagine a Pond. It's still. It's quiet. But because it doesn't move, every bit of debris that falls into it—every dead leaf, every handful of dust, every piece of trash just stays there. It sinks to the bottom. Over time, the water gets cloudy. Then it gets thick. Then it starts to smell. The pond eventually stops being "water" and becomes a stagnant record of every bad thing that ever fell into it.

Most men live like ponds.

- Someone insults you at work? **You hold it.** It sinks to the bottom and rots.
- A business deal falls through? **You let it cloud your view.** You stop trusting.
- A partner betrays you? **You let it turn your whole heart stagnant**. Eventually, you aren't "you" anymore; you're just a collection of every grudge and failure you've ever refused to let go of.

Now, look at the River. The same trash falls into the river. The same dead leaves, the same mud. But the river is moving. It accepts what falls in, but it doesn't keep it. It has a current. It has a purpose. It carries the debris downstream, and a mile later, the water is clear again.

The conscious man doesn't ask the world to stop dropping leaves into his water. He just builds a current so strong that nothing has the chance to settle and rot.

How the Other Wealths Feed the Flow

This "flow" isn't some mystical magic trick. It's an engineering feat built from the other fifteen wealths. This is why they are a single system.

- **A Steady Mind** is your riverbed. It gives you direction. Without a bed, the water just spills out into a chaotic, muddy mess.

- **Wisdom** is knowing the currents. You learn to bend around the rocks instead of crashing into them.
- **Strength** is the force of the flow itself. It's the grit to keep moving when the path gets narrow and dark.
- **Truthfulness** is the clarity of the water. Lies are like silt; they muddy everything up until you can't see where you're going.
- **Health** keeps the system pure. It's hard to have a "clear" mind when your body is inflamed and screaming for attention.

When even one of these wealths fails, the water slows down. The sediment starts to settle. You start to become a pond again.

Moving from Container to Current

If you feel like you're stagnating, if you feel the "stink" of old regrets or the weight of expectations that haven't been met, you have to get the water moving again.

1. **Separate the Event from the Story** Pain is the leaf falling into the water. It's a fact. It's a feeling. It hurts. **Suffering is the story you tell about the leaf.** It's the "Why does this always happen to me?" or "I'll never recover from this." Feel the pain. Acknowledge it. But for the love of your own sanity, do not crown it. Don't make it your king. Let it move.
2. **Lower the "Should" Fences** This isn't about having low standards; it's about **Radical Acceptance.** Hold yourself to a high standard, but stop demanding that the world follows your script. Your script is just a suggestion. When life ignores it, don't take it personally. It's just the wind.
3. **Move the Body to Move the Mind** Sadness and suffering love stillness. They thrive when you are slumped on a couch or staring at a screen. Physical motion, a heavy lift, a long walk, or even cleaning your desk, creates an "internal current." Action is the

enemy of stagnation. If you cannot think your way out, work your way out.

4. **Be the Witness, Not the Victim** When something hurts, try to look at it as if it's happening to a character in a book. *"Okay, I'm feeling betrayal right now. It's heavy. It's hot. It's here."* By witnessing it without "clinging" to it, you stop being the container and start being the course of water.

The Sea Doesn't Ask Questions

In the end, A Life Without Suffering isn't about being a robot. It's about being renewable.

You are not what happened to you ten years ago. You aren't even what happened to you ten minutes ago. You are the space through which those things pass. The pond collects; the river renews.

Your choice every single morning is whether you will be a container for your past or a current for your future. Build your other forms of wealth, your health, your honesty, and your friendships, because they are the "engines" that keep the water moving.

When the world tries to muddy your view or drop its trash into your heart, remember: You are not a pond. You are a force of nature. Keep moving. The sea doesn't care how many rocks were in the river's way; it only cares that the river arrived.

◆◆◆

You are not what happens to you.
You are the space it passes through.
Do not build a fence where a river should flow.

THE PRICE OF A LARGER LIFE

On Risk & Sacrifice

A man's true worth isn't found in the polished exterior of a "safe" life. It isn't measured by the absence of conflict or the stability of his surroundings. Instead, it is measured by the weight of what he is willing to put on the line for a life that actually resonates with his soul. We look at a man and see his house or his title, but the real story is written in the risks he took, and the ones he refused to take.

But we have to be honest: **"Risk" is one of the most misunderstood words in our language.**

We live in a culture that often confuses the adrenaline of a gambler with the courage of a leader. We applaud the man who bets the farm on a whim and happens to win, while we ignore the thousands who vanish into the shadows after lighting their futures on fire for a temporary rush. That isn't bravery. That is a form of self-sabotage.

Recklessness is a debt that your future self will eventually be forced to repay, and the interest rates are soul-crushing.

True masculinity isn't built on blind leaps into the dark. It thrives on calculated risk. Being "calculated" doesn't mean you are governed by fear or that you're a bean-counter of the spirit. It means you are brave enough to be honest. It means you have sat in the silence, taken a hard look at your life, and weighed your responsibilities. You've looked at the faces of your children, your partner, and the people who rely on you, and you've asked yourself: *"If I move, will the ground hold?"*

You don't try to weather a hurricane when you know the foundation of your house is already crumbling. You fix the foundation first. That foundation is built from what I call your **Quieter Wealths:**

- **Wisdom:** The capacity to see the recurring patterns of life instead of just reacting to your current mood.
- **Internal Strength:** A nervous system that can sit with uncertainty without reaching for a distraction or collapsing into panic.
- **Vitality**: Health that provides the long-term endurance required for a marathon, not just the flashy bursts of a sprint.

When these internal pillars are weak, your own mind becomes your worst enemy. It begins to lie to you. It magnifies every small shadow into a monster; it dresses up your cowardice and calls it "logic." It convinces you that staying small and blending into the crowd is the only way to survive. It tells you to live like a sheep because a sheep's life has no cliffs to fall from.

But we often forget: **A sheep's life also has no horizon.**

Is that what it means to be a man? To simply exist? No. That is merely survival inside a fence you've stopped noticing.

Why Take the Risk?

If safety is so seductive, why bother risking anything at all?

Because life was never meant to be a pile of coins you guard until you die. Life is an energy meant to be expanded. It is about increasing your capacity to contribute, to build, and to protect. Risk isn't about the "thrill" of the fall; it's about the necessity of growth.

A man who never leaves the safety of the pot never learns how big the world actually is. He never feels the friction of reality. And make no mistake: **Friction is the only thing that forges depth in a human soul.**

However, this expansion requires a payment. That payment is Sacrifice. There is no neutral gear in life. Every path you choose requires you to kill off another version of yourself.

Think about a man standing at a crossroads, the wind hitting his face:

- **Road A** is the Familiar: The steady paycheck, the predictable routine, the comfort of knowing exactly what tomorrow looks like.
- **Road B** is the Uncertain: The business idea he can't stop thinking about, the creative calling, the "thing" he knows he was built to do but has no guarantee of success.

If he takes the uncertain road, he sacrifices his comfort. He gives up the luxury of "off-hours" and the soothing warmth of a guaranteed salary. But if he chooses the familiar road, he sacrifices something far more precious: **The man he was supposed to become.** He sacrifices the legacy of his own potential. He kills the version of himself that could have built something lasting.

Both roads cost him everything. The tragedy is that most people think only one road has a price tag.

Common vs. Conscious Masculinity

This is where we see the divide in the modern world. Today, "starting a business" or "taking a risk" is often just a trendy way of seeking instant gratification. It's gambling dressed up in a suit.

A true venture, a true act of masculinity, is an extension of a man's character. It is his discipline, his sense of justice, and his internal order taking physical form in the world. It solves a real problem for real people.

- **The Common Man** is obsessed with the outcome. He only cares about winning or losing, the scoreboard, and the external validation.
- **The Conscious Man** looks deeper. He sees the two sacrifices laid out on the table and makes a deliberate choice.

On one side is the **Sacrifice of Comfort.** It is loud, it is immediate, and it hurts today. On the other side is the **Sacrifice of Potential.** It is quiet. It doesn't hurt today. It waits. It accumulates slowly over decades until it turns into a heavy, suffocating regret that haunts your final years.

The Silent Trap of Dependency

To even be capable of making this choice, a man must first be free.

Dependency is the silent killer of courage. Debt, bloated lifestyles, and the desperate need for social validation are psychological chains. They turn a man into a hostage who has convinced himself that his captivity is actually "responsibility."

When you are one missed paycheck away from total ruin, you cannot take a calculated risk. You can only react. You aren't "choosing" growth; you are just trying not to drown. True risk capacity is built in the years of quiet discipline before the crossroads ever appears.

It is built by simplifying your life so your courage has room to breathe. It is built by choosing clarity over impulse and steadiness over anxiety. When your life isn't weighed down by unnecessary needs, the crossroads stops being a terrifying jump and starts being an honest question: **"Where am I meant to grow next?"**

The Only Real Choice

The instruction for a meaningful life isn't complicated, but it is incredibly demanding.

You must live now as the man capable of handling freedom later. You don't wait for a "sign" or for someone to give you permission to be great. You become disciplined today because disorder makes future courage impossible.

This isn't just "preparing" for risk. This is the risk. You are risking the identity of the "safe, predictable man" for the identity of the "capable, dangerous-but-disciplined man." You are letting go of the comfort of being understood by everyone.

The pattern is simple, but severe:

- **Build your foundation** (The Quieter Wealths).
- **Break the chains** (Kill the debt, the ego, and the need for approval).
- **Choose your sacrifice.**

If you choose growth, you will lose sleep. You will be mocked. You will fail, and people will see it. But if you choose comfort, you will lose that spark in your eyes. You will feel a quiet shrinking of your spirit every time you realize the days are just repeating themselves.

Both paths will cost you your life. **Only one path gives you a life worth paying for.**

Choose with your eyes wide open.

◆◆◆

Every man stands at a crossroads:
Sacrifice comfort, or sacrifice potential.
One costs you comfort.
The other costs you yourself.

WHY YOU CANNOT BUILD ALONE

A trust, values & friendship

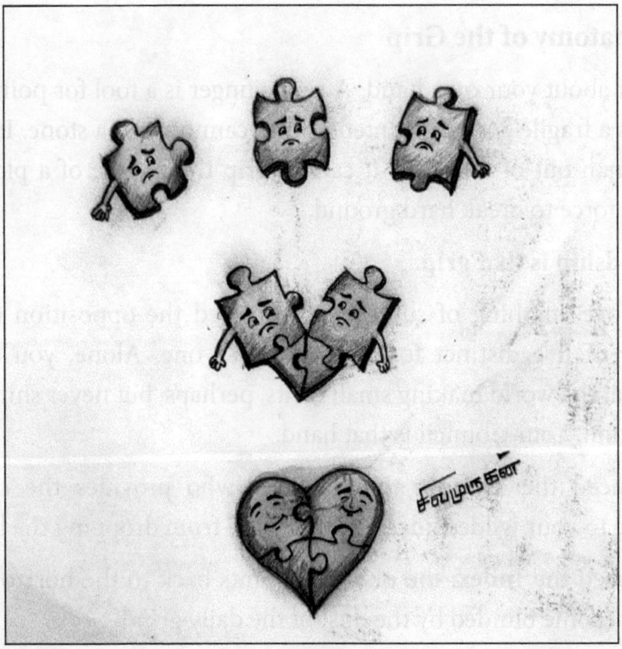

You wake up with a vision so heavy it feels like a physical ache in your chest. It's a stubborn, restless will to change the world or at least the corner of it you occupy. But as soon as you take that first real step, the adrenaline of the "idea" fades, and you hit a wall of cold reality: Ambition is heavy. It is a bone-deep, exhausting weight that was never designed to be carried by a single pair of shoulders.

We have been poisoned by the myth of the "Lone Wolf." We idolize the man standing solitary on the mountain, bearing the weight of the world like Atlas. But that mountain is a lonely place to die. If you look closely at the men who actually shifted the tectonic plates of history, you don't see a solo act. You see a man held upright by a Council. True builders don't work with a single finger; they build with a grip, a team, and the kind of stubborn soil that only stays put when it's packed down by the feet of brothers.

The Anatomy of the Grip

Think about your own hand. A single finger is a tool for pointing, or perhaps a fragile gesture of intent. But it cannot hold a stone. It cannot pull a man out of a trench. It cannot grip the handle of a plow with enough force to break hard ground.

Friendship is that grip.

To move anything of substance, you need the opposition and the synergy of five distinct forces working as one. Alone, you are just poking at the world making small dents, perhaps, but never shifting the foundation. Your Council is that hand.

You need the **Thumb**: the stabilizer who provides the counter-pressure to your wildest ideas, keeping you from dropping the ball.

You need the **Index**: the one who points back to the horizon when you've become blinded by the dust of the daily grind.

You need the **Middle**: the raw, unyielding strength that simply shows up when the work gets ugly.

Without these distinct voices, your ambition is just a scream in a vacuum. With them, it becomes a fist that can break through walls or a palm that can build a sanctuary.

The Kingdom and the Quiet Court

You are the "Quiet King" of your own life, the sovereign over your household, your craft, and your word. But the mark of a failed king is the one who tries to be his own general, his own treasurer, and his own palace guard. That man doesn't end up powerful; he ends up hollowed out by exhaustion.

True friendship is the safe delegation of your soul.

It means trusting someone else to watch the gates while you sleep. It means having a Treasurer of your energy, someone who looks you in the eye and tells you that you are overleveraged, that you are spending your spirit on things that don't matter. It's having a Commander who calls you out when you're leaning into the soft comfort of your own excuses.

This isn't "networking." It's survival. You borrow their clarity when your vision is clouded by fatigue, and in the lean seasons, they borrow yours. You go further not because you are faster, but because you aren't carrying the entire armory on your own back.

The Anchor in the Wind of Praise

The moment you start to succeed, a new predator appears: the "Yes-Man." These are people who clothe their own hunger in the language of flattery. They want to be near your fire, so they tell you exactly what you want to hear.

When the world starts calling you "excellent," the only person who can keep **you human is the friend who cannot be bought.** This is the man who needs absolutely nothing from you. Because he has no stake in your ego, he has the terrifying freedom to tell you the truth. He is the anchor that keeps your feet on the dirt when the wind of your own pride would pull you into the clouds. To find a friend like this, you must first be a man like this. You must refuse to put a price on your loyalty or your honesty.

The Practical Architecture of a Legacy

This isn't about being "nice" or having "good vibes." This is cold-blooded, practical architecture.

- **The Solo Builder:** His first victories are loud and flashy, but his failures are absolute. Because no one was there to challenge his plans, pride grew where friction should have been. He builds a house that looks great from the street, but the moment the ground tremors, the cracks show. No one was there to hold the beams while the roof was raised.

- **The Council-Builder:** He chooses steadiness over spectacle. He invites "demanding architects" into his life—men who will test his plans, break his certainties, and sharpen his tools. His victories are quieter, but they are built of reinforced steel.

How do you become this man? You start by being the land for someone else's river. You offer your own roughness as well as your polish. You find the men who don't rush to compliment you, but who rush to engage with the work you are actually doing.

Ambition is a heavy burden. Do not pretend you are a god who can lift it alone. Assemble your Hand. Rule with a Court. Flow within your River. Only then will the work you begin today have the structural integrity to outlive you. This brotherhood is the alloy in your steel. It is the reason you dare to become more than just a man standing alone in the dark.

Protect this wealth. Cultivate it with the same ferocity you bring to your work, because when the world eventually strips away the titles, the Council is the only thing that will be real.

◆ ◆ ◆

A king without a court is a servant to his own crown.
A river without banks is a flood.
Build boundaries that hold your flow
not cages that stop it.

THE CHOICE

Sacrifice or Alignment?

There is a specific kind of pain that most men are never taught to name. It isn't the sharp sting of a physical wound or the dull ache of a bruise after a fall. It is much quieter than that. It's a persistent, rhythmic grind in the ribs, a slow, almost imperceptible wearing away of hope. It grows in the dark spaces of your life, fed by every moment you choose to put your soul on hold for a version of "comfort" that never actually fills the void.

You do what you were told to do. You protect. You provide. You solve. You become the man who fixes the leak and pays the mortgage. But somewhere along that dusty road, you wake up and realize you have handed over the one thing you promised you'd never lose: **yourself**.

We were all raised on a very tidy, very honorable rule: *A man provides. A man protects. A man solves problems.* That rule isn't a lie, but it is dangerously incomplete. There is a deep, noble beauty in the instinct to keep your family warm and safe. It builds the foundation of trust upon which a home is raised. But a subtle, lethal confusion often slips in through the cracks. We start to mistake "providing for others" with "disappearing into the role of the provider."

One is a duty that ennobles you. The other is a form of self-erasure that eventually leaves you hollow.

You can find the truth of your own situation by asking one gut-level question: **Does the life I am building actually have room for the person I am becoming?**

If the answer is "no," you are drifting toward a quiet, middle-aged tragedy. You are burying your own spirit so the household ledger stays in the black. You buy the bigger SUV to silence a feeling of inadequacy; you accept the safe, soul-crushing job because it feels "responsible"; you swallow excuses about what your family "needs" to keep the peace.

But every concession you make takes a bite out of your fire. The loan you think you're paying off with money is actually being settled with your curiosity, your joy, and the creative projects that died before they could even breathe. **Resentment is the interest rate on a life you didn't choose.**

The Danger of the Hollow Man

Duty is not your enemy. The enemy is the unconscious trade-off. You tell yourself, "If I chase what I love and fail, my family suffers." So, you choose the steady paycheck and accept the slow death of a life half-lived.

But look at your children. Look at your partner. Do they really demand that you stop being a human being? Or do they actually need your presence, your vitality, and a future where everyone has permission to grow?

There is a world of difference between being the man who sits at the head of the table and being the hollow shell of a man who merely delivers the plates. **A hollow man cannot hold a family together; he can only finance its existence**. And a family doesn't want a financier—they want a father and a husband who is actually alive.

Marriage or Procurement?

This is where the quality of your partnership becomes the ultimate filter for your life.

A healthy, conscious partner doesn't see your personal dreams as a threat to the grocery budget. She knows that when you are on fire, the whole house stays warm. She doesn't ask you to give up your soul so she can feel "safe." Instead, she asks: *"How do we build a life where there is room for both of us to breathe?"*

She becomes a multiplier. Her steadiness gives your vision a place to land. Her practical sense keeps the ship upright while you're learning to steer through the storm. That is alignment. That is the definition of a "power couple."

But you have to be honest: If your partner's primary language is a never-ending list of demands—for a bigger house, a more impressive title, more "proof" to show the neighbors—then you need to pause. You aren't in a marriage; you're trapped in a procurement contract. In that contract, love is reframed as an obligation. You are valued for what you bring, not for who you are. Eventually, you'll wake up surprised by how heavy your heart feels when you speak the name of the person you once adored.

Needs vs. The Social Vaccine

Why do we feel this crushing pressure? Usually, it's because we confuse a Need with what I call a **Social Vaccine.**

- **A Need is sacred:** Food, a roof, healthcare, an education. This is the soil of life. A man works for these things with pride.
- **A Social Vaccine** is a status symbol: It's the $800 car payment, the designer labels, or the oversized wedding. It's an expensive purchase meant to "numb" the shame of comparison. It's a way to silence the neighbors' judgment.

One of these secures your life. The other tries to patch an internal insecurity with external noise. **Provide the need. Transcend the vaccine.**

The Path Back to the Light

If you realize you've become the "hollow provider," you don't run away. You don't blow up your life. You lead your way out of the trap with clarity.

1. **Speak the Raw Truth:** Sit your partner down and tell the truth. Say: *"I want to build a life rich in purpose, not just things. I need to bring my whole self to our home, but right now, I'm disappearing. I need us to figure out a way back."* This isn't a complaint; it's an invitation to a shared vision.
2. **Use Honest Scripts:** When you make a trade, name it. *"I will handle the bills, but I need two nights a week where my time is sacred for my work."* or *"I'm taking a risk on this project for six months. Can we tighten our belts together to see if it has legs?"* Clear language prevents silent resentment from taking root.
3. **The Small Win Plan:** Sit down and write three things. One sacrifice that buys you real safety (like killing a debt), one investment in your future growth (like a course or a side hustle), and one small, free thing that keeps the joy in your home (like a Saturday morning walk).

If your partner resists, it's usually because of fear—not malice. Most demands for "more" are actually secret pleas for security. Address the fear. Show her the plan. Don't promise miracles; promise transparency.

The Lamp of Dignity

Remember this: You attract the energy you put out. If you are a man who is clear, steady, and building toward something real, you won't end up with a partner who only cares about the glitter. A mismatch in your relationship often reflects a mismatch inside your own heart.

Ask yourself: *Have I been clear about who I am? Or have I been pretending to be a "safe man" to avoid the hard conversations?*

A great marriage isn't two people staring at each other in a vacuum. It's two people standing shoulder-to-shoulder, looking at the same horizon. The load is shared. The vision is shared. Love becomes a joint mission rather than a creditor's ledger.

In the ancient wisdom of the 16 Wealths, A Loving Partner and Righteous Children are listed right alongside material success. But those wealths cannot bloom in a house built on a foundation of resentment. They require a man who is present, awake, and vital—not just a man who is "employed."

There will be seasons where you must sacrifice. A father might sell his most prized possession to pay for his child's medicine. That is the beauty of a man's heart. But sacrifice is a choice, and it is temporary. Disappearance is a habit, and it is permanent.

Do not confuse the two.

Hold your dignity like a fragile lamp in a dark wind. Dignity isn't arrogance; it's coherence. It means you refuse to be someone else's safety net at the cost of your own soul. The greatest protection you can give your family isn't a bigger house or a fancy car. It is the example of a life lived whole, where your work feeds your spirit and your presence feeds your home.

Be the man who lives for them, not just the man who dies for them. That is the only gift that truly lasts.

◆ ◆ ◆

Alignment begins within.
If you are not becoming who you are,
you cannot bring who you are
to those you love.

THE MIRROR OF THE SOUL

A Loving Partner

Strength can be built through discipline. Wealth can be earned through sweat. Wisdom often comes through failure. But there is one form of wealth that cannot be grown alone. It only appears in the presence of another person.

The ancients called this wealth a loving partner, someone faithful, kind, and steady. For many men today, this does not feel like a reward. It feels like a risk.

Listen to the small, private fears that rattle in the back of your mind. *"What if she only wants the security I provide, not me?" "What if I'm not enough and she leaves?"* And the loudest, most cynical fear of our era: *"What if she takes half of everything I've bled to build?"*

These aren't just "insecure thoughts." They sit in the chest like weight. They are fed by stories of courtrooms, broken homes, and men hollowed out by systems that promised unity and delivered conflict. But there is a harder truth beneath these fears. Often, they say more about how you understand yourself than about the woman you imagine.

If you want a form of wealth that no judge can divide, you must first understand what marriage actually is.

It is not two roommates splitting rent, and it is not merely a legal signature. It is the point at which two lives become a single entity. The separate borders of "I" and "You" dissolve, and a "We" takes their place.

If we think about it logically, we are able to live in harmony with another person in two broad scenarios.

In one, both individuals are inwardly settled and steady. They are not driven by unchecked desire or fragile ego. Because there is little inner turbulence, living together feels natural and requires minimal effort.

In the other, both individuals are clearly defined. They know what they value, what they seek, and what they will not compromise. They choose each other because their inner direction aligns. Here, harmony does not come from flexibility, but from moving toward the same horizon.

The Garden of Peace

This is where most of us will fall, and it is a noble, beautiful place to be. This is the marriage of shared trajectory. It works because both of you want the same kind of life. Your ambitions do not compete. They reinforce each other. One person's strength supports the other's momentum.

This is why ancient cultures paid close attention to patterns, temperaments, and compatibility through astrology. It was not superstition. It was recognition that misaligned values eventually create friction that no affection can absorb.

There is real wealth in this peace. It creates stable ground where children can grow without constant ideological tension. If you find someone who walks with you through hardship and shares your joy without resentment, do not dismiss that comfort. Peace is not ordinary. It is a luxury.

The Mountain of Growth

There is another path, far rarer and far more demanding.

This is not about matching personalities or finding someone who completes you. It is about meeting someone who refuses to let you hide.

In ancient texts, love is most often described this way, not as emotional comfort or mutual gratification, but as a force that reveals truth. The logic is simple. You can give up what you do not deeply desire. But you cannot trade the love of the soul for convenience without losing yourself.

This kind of relationship shines a light into every corner you have avoided. It exposes fear, insecurity, pride, and self-deception with unflinching clarity. There is no hiding behind roles, titles, income, or charm. You must stand before another human being without armor, without performance, and without excuse.

The soul seeks freedom, but the mind is often bound by habit, memory, and old survival patterns. When deep clarity confronts unresolved conditioning, friction is inevitable. The mind resists. It reaches for comfort. It urges a return to familiar ground where nothing is questioned.

Unless both people are committed to truth rather than comfort, they will pull away. The vulnerability required here feels threatening because ego has nowhere to hide. Shame surfaces. Insecurity surfaces. Everything false is forced into the open. This is why such unions are rare.

A classical example often referenced in ancient tradition is the union of Sivan and Parvati. Both underwent deep inner refinement before union. Their bond was not based on convenience or social logic, but on shared inner alignment and purpose.

Beyond Romantic Fantasy

In the modern world, it is easy to look at ancient archetypes and say, *"They chose each other. Why shouldn't we just follow our hearts?"*

But this misses the point.

Those unions were not romantic fantasies. They were the result of intense inner work. Nothing was bypassed. Nothing was borrowed. Because of that preparation, the union produced wisdom and stability rather than chaos.

Now consider the opposite pattern.

Imagine a powerful king driven by ego who enters a union with a partner driven by unchecked desire. Neither has done the internal work. From that union comes a child carrying strength without restraint and hunger without clarity. Instead of serving the people, he exploits them. Instead of protecting life, he consumes it.

Ancient texts return to this warning again and again through stories of unions between sages and asuras, where imbalance grows so severe it threatens the world itself. Power amplifies whatever it touches. Without clarity and discipline, it multiplies harm.

When it is merely two desires colliding, it is not a union. It is an explosion, and its damage always spreads beyond the couple. The lesson is uncompromising. Our purpose here is to gain clarity and take responsibility for our actions. **Nothing is too late. Purpose begins with clarity and responsibility.**

The Modern Mistake: Ego vs. Soul

Today, many want the status of a king and the freedom of an ascetic. A man marries for beauty. A woman marries for security. Ego remains intact. Desire remains unquestioned. Nothing is stripped away. Everything is stacked higher.

When two egos marry, the relationship becomes a transaction. When the transaction fails, it ends in litigation. **When two Souls marry, the impulse to sue dissolves, because they no longer experience life as "mine versus yours," but as "ours."**

Fear of Marriage

Think of fire and water. You may be fire, direct and transforming. She may be water, fluid and cleansing. Fire fears being extinguished. Water fears being overheated.

When both remain open, each learns from the other. Strength becomes balanced. The direct can learn patience. The cautious can learn courage. The emotionally sensitive can learn practicality, and the practical can learn emotional intelligence. The outcome depends not on difference, but on how open both of you are within the relationship.

How to Build the Sanctuary

Whether you are in the Garden or on the Mountain, the work of building the vessel is the same:

Be Trustworthy First: Before you ask if you can trust her with your money, ask if you are the kind of man a trustworthy woman would choose. Make your word your bond.

Drop the "Type": Stop looking for a social category and start looking for a person. Love is not an idea; it is a human being.

Create a Sanctuary: The world is a marketplace of judgment. Your marriage should be the opposite: a place to lay down your armor. Never weaponize vulnerability.

Burn the Ledger: Sacrifice is required. But if you keep a tally of what you gave, the gift curdles into a debt. A covenant of generosity cannot fail.

The Final Alignment

There is a final truth: Marriage is the atmosphere in which your children will grow. A child is a sponge for the energy of the home. They learn more from the silent repetition of their mother's values and her daily choices than from any sermon you give.

If you are a man on a mission, seeking a life of purpose, you cannot walk in alignment with a heart that is anchored in the constant hunger for worldly status or desires. To choose a partner who seeks the world while you seek the light is to invite a permanent friction into the very soil of your home.

Seek a partner whose character can carry the weight of your mission. When you choose a woman of purpose, respect is not an obligation. It arises naturally from who she is. In her, you find not a dependent, but a fellow guardian of the life you are building.

Whether you find the peaceful Garden or the challenging Mountain, do not marry out of fear of being alone. Marry when you are ready to share. When the connection is true, she is not just a comfort; she is a multiplier. She makes your courage braver, your wisdom sharper, and your peace deeper.

Walk the path together. Build a union that no court can unravel and a wealth that no ledger can measure.

Unconditional love is rare and costly, and only a few can carry it.

Important Note:

Marriage involves another human being who is on their own journey of growth, confusion, and change. You cannot fully depend on another person to carry your expectations or move exactly as you wish, just as you yourself cannot always live up to your own promises. Expecting someone else to choose or behave according to your inner script is unrealistic.

The task, then, is not control but openness. If a deep connection appears, meet it honestly and walk it with care. If it does not, continue your own journey with integrity. Either way, your responsibility remains the same: clarity, growth, and responsibility for your own life.

◆ ◆ ◆

Two egos marry and keep score.
Two souls marry and become one.
The first is a contract.
The second is a covenant.

THE RIGHTEOUS CHILD

On Raising Stones, Not Shadows

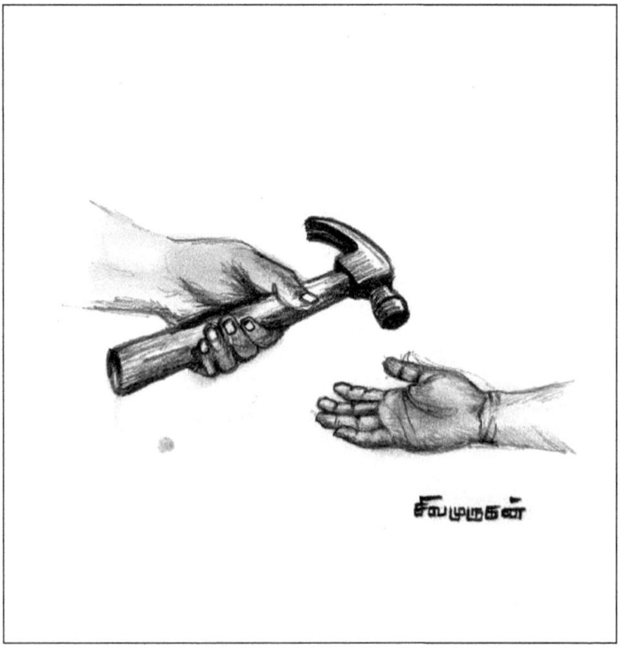

We have spent our time talking about the wealth you build with your hands, the friends you choose to keep close, and the partner who walks the long road beside you. But there is one specific form of wealth that is unlike any other. It is the only thing you own that you do not actually keep. You release it into a future you will never see. The ancients had a name for this. They called it Righteous Children.

In our modern world, we have twisted the meaning of this word until it is unrecognizable. We have come to believe that righteousness is simply obedience or a set of moral lessons drilled into a child like a military exercise. We think a righteous child is one who follows the rules and avoids bringing shame to the family name. But that is a hollow definition. A righteous child is not a well behaved shadow of their parents. A righteous child is a self governing soul. They are a human being capable of meeting the world with clarity, courage, and a solid character long after your voice has faded from their ears.

This is where the great modern failure begins. We have confused provision with protection. we have convinced ourselves that giving a child comfort is the same as giving them strength. It is actually the opposite. Comfort often acts as a slow poison to the spirit.

The Two Inheritances

Every father leaves behind two distinct legacies, and they rarely look the same.

First, there is the Dead Inheritance. This is the money, the property, or the safe job arranged through a network of contacts. This kind of wealth is static. It can be spent, it can be lost, or it can be squandered by someone who never learned its value. It carries a heavy, unspoken message: You are not enough on your own without what I have left for you.

Second, there is the Living Inheritance. This is resilience. This is discernment. It is the hard won ability to stand back up after a devastating fall and the courage to look a difficult truth in the eye. This inheritance is dynamic. It does not shrink when it is used; it grows. It whispers a different message: You are capable because of the strength I have helped you find within yourself.

Most men spend their entire lives obsessed with the first, while completely neglecting the second. They work themselves to the bone to ensure their child's comfort, but they do nothing to ensure their child's competence.

The Forge of Experience

Consider a simple truth: if every lesson worth knowing were written down in a book, would you have actually learned it? No. Words are just maps. Experience is the actual territory. You do not learn the mechanics of walking by reading a manual on balance. You learn it by the feeling of the sidewalk hitting your knees and the grit it takes to stand up and try again.

Yet, we treat our children as if they are made of thin glass. We move the stones out of their path so they never trip. We jump in to solve their conflicts before they even have a chance to speak. We hand them the answers before they have even felt the heavy weight of the question. In doing this, what are we actually protecting them from? We are protecting them from the only thing that can make them strong.

A stone in a field does not become a deity by sitting untouched in the sun. It must be struck by the craftsman's chisel. It must be ground by the wheel and polished by the heat of friction. Your child's soul is that stone. Struggle is the chisel. Failure is the wheel. Responsibility is the polish. To withhold these things from them is not an act of love. It is an act of cowardice. It is your own fear of seeing them hurt or your own anxiety about their stumbles dressed up in the clothing of care.

The Player and The Witness

Imagine two boys at a game. The Witness sits in the front row and watches every play. He learns the rules perfectly. He can critique the players and he knows every statistic and strategy. But his feet have never felt the heat of the turf. His lungs have never burned in the final minute of a tie game. His hands have never shaken with the weight of a loss that was entirely his fault.

Then there is the Player. He is out on the field. He falls down. He gets scored against. He loses far more often than he wins. But the Player learns things the Witness can never know. He learns to read the field.

He learns to trust his own limbs. He learns how to carry the quiet weight of defeat and the internal fire of resolve.

The Witness has knowledge, but the Player has wisdom. Most modern children are being raised as Witnesses. We give them a front row seat to a life we are living for them. Then we act surprised when they turn out to be anxious, entitled, and lost when the game finally demands their own feet upon the field.

How to Forge a Living Inheritance

The work of a father is not to build a castle for his child and lock them inside for safety. It is to give them the tools, show them where the quarry is, and have the heart to stand back as they build their own.

1. **Replace certainty with challenge.**

   Do not say: I will handle it. Instead, ask them: How will you handle it? When they face a conflict at school or a failed test, do not rush to fix the situation. Guide them to find the lesson in the rubble. Let them sit with the temporary discomfort of not knowing the answer. That is exactly where resourcefulness is born.

2. **Give responsibility, not an allowance.**

   Money that is given freely only teaches a child how to consume. Money that is earned through a real contribution teaches them value. Let them contribute to the life of the house in ways that actually matter. These should not be chores done for pocket money, but duties that uphold the family. Let them feel the weight of real consequence when they fail to show up.

3. **Normalize failure as data.**

   When they fall, do not tell them it doesn't matter. It does matter. Instead, ask: What did this teach you? You must separate the failure from the person. A failed attempt is not a failed child. It is simply feedback. Treat these moments as the most valuable curriculum they will ever have.

4. **Model the path, do not just preach it.**

Your child will never remember your long lectures on the importance of honesty. They will, however, remember the time you went back into a store to return the extra change a clerk gave you by mistake. They will learn courage by watching you face a personal loss with dignity. They learn respect by watching the way you speak to their mother when things are tense. Your character is their first and most lasting textbook.

5. **Loosen your grip.**

The ancient stories tell us that Murugan, the god of wisdom and war, was not raised in the suffocating comfort of a palace. He was sent out into the world to be forged by direct encounter. His strength was not in spite of this separation; it was because of it. You do not have to send your child away, but you must give them increasing degrees of sovereignty. Let them choose, let them risk, and let them own the outcome sooner rather than later.

The Only Righteousness That Lasts

A righteous child is not one who never makes a mistake. It is one who knows exactly how to return to their integrity after they have failed. It is not a child who is shielded from the world, but one who has been prepared to meet it head on.

Your greatest gift to them is not a safety net. It is trust. It is the trust that they can learn, that they can endure, and that they can rise on their own. When you hoard money because you think they cannot survive without it, you are not loving them. You are confessing your own lack of faith in the human being you have raised.

Instead, invest everything in their resilience. Give them the Living Inheritance. Let them be struck by the chisel. Let them be smoothed by the wheel. Let them be polished by the friction of a real life. Then, one day when you are gone, they will not stand before the world holding a bag of your coins. They will stand holding something that can never be taken away: their own forged character. That is the only wealth that never depreciates. It is the final and greatest test of a conscious man. It is not about what he built for himself, but about who he raised to build a better world after he is gone.

◆◆◆

You are not building a castle for them to live in.
You are giving them tools to build their own.
One is a gift that shelters.
The other is a skill that liberates.

THE UNBREAKABLE WORD

On Truthfulness

Long before we are measured by the weight of our purses or the reach of our names, we are weighed by something more elemental: the resonance of our breath when it becomes a promise. The ancients understood this with a clarity we often lack today. They spoke of Satyam or Vaimai (truthfulness) not as a rigid moral ornament worn for display, but as a living form of wealth.

Why? Because your word is the primary currency of your character. It is the first thing others touch when they encounter your soul. In a world of shifting shadows, your word is the light by which people navigate your intentions.

Keeping your word may look like simple discipline from the outside, but its roots reach into the bedrock of the spirit. It is an act of **Alignment**—the quiet, sacred matching of what you say, what you do, and who you fundamentally are. This alignment is more grueling than any physical workout and more complex than any high-stakes negotiation. It is difficult because life is a moving river; the man who makes a promise at dawn is rarely the same man who must fulfill it at dusk.

You vow to run each morning, and a fever arrives to test you. You promise to help a friend, and an emergency pulls you elsewhere. That narrow and often painful gap between the making of a promise and the effort to keep it is where character is formed, tempered into steel or reduced to ash.

The Three Fractures of the Broken Word

Many dismiss a broken promise as a minor lapse, a mere "human" error. It is far more destructive than that. When you betray your word, you initiate a triple collapse:

1. **The External Erosion (The Death of Trust)** Every time you falter, you teach the world that your "yes" is actually a "perhaps." You do not just disappoint others; you diminish their sense of safety. They begin to reserve themselves, withholding their true hearts because they can no longer rely on your gravity. You become a slow drip on the stone of their certainty until, eventually, the stone splits.
2. **The Internal Fracture (The Divided Self)** A broken promise creates a schism within. One part of you spoke with authority; another part disobeyed with cowardice. This split breeds a restless, haunted mind that no longer believes in its own power. You become a man who negotiates with himself, and that inward bargaining is the prelude to a life of mediocrity and doubt.

3. **The Foundation's Collapse (The Weakening of Wealth)** Relationships are the true infrastructure of a meaningful life, and they cannot stand on shifting sand. Friendships wither when they must be maintained by excuses. Partnerships buckle under the weight of "reading between the lines." Children, the keenest observers of all, learn that character is optional if the cost of integrity is too high. A broken word is never an isolated crack; it is a fault line running through the foundation of your entire house.

The Sanctuary of the Kept Word

Now, imagine the alternative. Consider the man whose word is an immutable law. He does not scatter promises like seeds in the wind; he plants them carefully, like oaks. When he speaks, the world adjusts to accommodate his intent.

The atmosphere around such a man is not filled with trophies, but with Safety. People reveal their true selves in his presence because they know his word will never be weaponized against their vulnerability. They bring him their fears and their grandest plans, knowing his "yes" is a refuge. In an age where opinions are loud and commitments are fluid, a man who keeps his word becomes an Anchor for everyone he touches.

The Discipline of the Unbreakable Word

This path does not require perfection, but it demands relentless intention. To live a life of Satyam, we must adopt specific practices that turn truthfulness into a living, breathing habit.

- **The Sacred Pause:** Before you commit, pause. Do not promise in the heat of passion, under the weight of social pressure, or in a fleeting moment of enthusiasm. Ask yourself: *"Can I honor this when I am exhausted, when I am busy, or when a more glittering opportunity calls?"* If the answer is not a resounding yes, offer a respectful no. A "no" delivered with honesty is a thousand times more honorable than a "yes" delivered with hesitation.

- **The Altar of Small Things:** Integrity is built in the mundane. Return the call when you said you would. Arrive five minutes early. Complete the trivial task you promised yourself you'd finish by sunset. These small victories wire the brain to recognize the sanctity of commitment. They train you to be a man of follow-through.
- **The Ritual of Repair:** Life is unpredictable. Occasionally, a promise will be broken by forces beyond your control—illness, tragedy, or honest failure. In these moments, your duty is not to hide, but to repair. Do not offer excuses; offer an explanation. Acknowledge the harm caused by your absence. Present a concrete plan to make amends. A promise honestly repaired can, paradoxically, build more trust than one kept without effort.
- **The North Star of Reputation:** Your image will fluctuate in the minds of others. But if you allow one question to guide your steps—*"Was I a man of my word?"*—your life will find its true north. Build your legacy on what you honor, not what you advertise. Skills and money may fade, but a reliable name echoes long after the man is gone.
- **The Architecture of Accountability:** Use the tools at your disposal. Write your promises down. Tell a witness. Set the reminder. These are not signs of weakness; they are the tools of the honest. By externalizing your intent, you protect yourself from the small, foggy betrayals that eventually lead to catastrophic faults.

The Final Mirror

Ultimately, your word is the mirror in which you view your own soul. Every promise kept is a stroke of the cloth, polishing that mirror until it reflects a man of substance. Every promise broken leaves a smudge, blurring the image until you no longer recognize the face staring back.

Start today. Make one small, private promise to yourself and keep it with everything you have. Then, make one promise to another person and fulfill it. Feel the quiet, unshakable solidity that begins to grow in the center of your chest. That calm is not an accident; it is the true wealth of a truthful life.

Keep your word. Be the man whose "yes" carries weight in the world. That is the only foundation upon which a life of true meaning can ever be built.

◆◆◆

A "yes" without weight is noise.
A "no" with respect is music.
Choose your notes carefully.
They compose the song of your character.

THE SCAFFOLD AND THE RIVER

Generosity

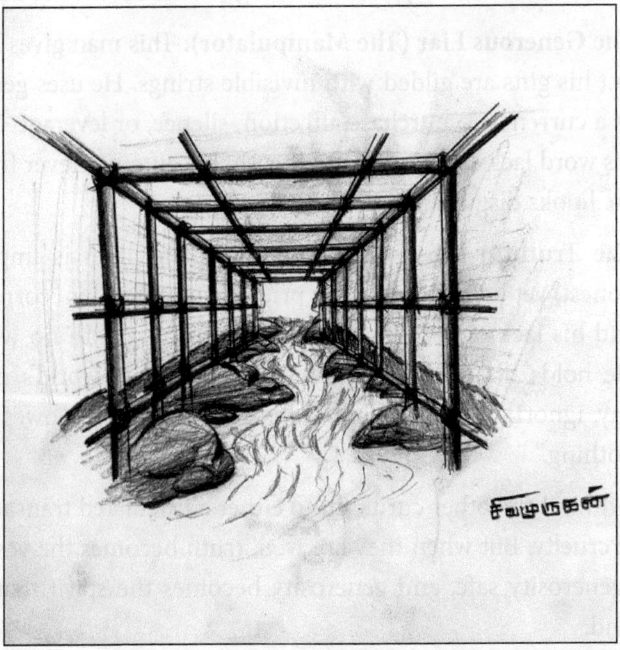

The Unbreakable Word is the integrity that turns a man into a sanctuary. But strength without warmth hardens into a monument. To measure a life more fully, you must also understand its essential twin: **The Open Hand.**

The ancients did not separate Truthfulness (Vaimai) and Generosity (Kodai) by mere whim. They understood them as the biological rhythm of the spirit—the inhale and the exhale. If truth is the spine that allows a man to stand tall, then generosity is the heartbeat that proves he is alive. One provides the structure; the other provides the pulse. Together, they create a human being who is solid without being cold, and expansive without being hollow.

The Architect of Shadows: The Miser and The Manipulator

When these two virtues are divorced, the human character begins to warp. Consider the archetypes that emerge in the absence of balance:

- **The Generous Liar (The Manipulator):** This man gives lavishly, but his gifts are gilded with invisible strings. He uses generosity as a currency to purchase affection, silence, or leverage. Because his word lacks a foundation of truth, his gifts are never free; they are hooks disguised as flowers.
- **The Truthful Miser (The Fortress):** This man is impeccably honest, yet he is a desert. He prides himself on his "correctness" and his lack of debt, but his life is a fortress with no windows. He holds his truth like a shield to keep the world's needs at bay, ignoring the suffering at his gate because he "owes no one nothing."

One without the other curdles into either a calculated transaction or a sterile cruelty. But when they are wed, truth becomes the vessel that makes generosity safe, and generosity becomes the spirit that makes truth kind.

The Architecture of the Pure Gift

When a man is known for his truth, his generosity lands with a unique, crystalline weight. A gift from a truthful man carries no "hidden invoice." The receiver does not have to scan the horizon for a favor to be returned or a price to be paid. Because the man's word is solid, the gift is finally allowed to be pure. Conversely, generosity softens the sharp edges of honesty. You no longer fling the truth like a spear to wound or to feel superior; you deliver it like bread. You speak the difficult word because you desire the other person's growth, not their diminishment.

In this union, your "no" becomes an act of respect, and your "yes" becomes a cornerstone upon which others can build their lives.

The Four Disciplines of the Open Hand

To live this duality requires more than a vague intention; it requires a daily practice of the soul.

1. **Incinerate the Internal Ledger** The moment you think, "I did this for them," you have stopped giving and started lending. To give like a human is to give like a river—flowing because that is your nature, not because you expect the sea to thank you. Delete the mental record of your kindnesses; only then can you remain free.
2. **Offer Bread, Not Spears** Before delivering a "hard truth," examine your tools. If you use honesty as a shield for your own irritation, you are wielding a spear. If you speak to nourish the other person's journey, you are offering bread. If the truth must cause pain, be the person who stays to help bind the wound.
3. **The Economy of the Sacred Yes** Do not use a "yes" to buy a temporary reputation for kindness. A truthful "no" is infinitely more compassionate than a "yes" born of cowardice that eventually rots into resentment. Guard your promises religiously so that when you do give your word, it is as tangible as gold.
4. **Invest Presence Over Pelf** Generosity is measured by what you sacrifice, and for most, time is more precious than money. To give a problem your checkbook is one thing; to give a person your undivided attention is another. Let your giving reveal your truth: give your presence to that which you claim to value.

The Final Mirror: The Scaffold and the River

You will know this alchemy is working within you when the world begins to respond in kind. People will no longer flinch when you speak the truth, for they know your heart is for them. You will find that you can give without the ego swelling, and receive gratitude without a sense of entitlement.

The final test is a simple reflection:

- Does your giving increase the receiver's freedom, or does it bind them to you?
- Does your truth make others feel safer in your presence, or does it make them feel small?

Build your character like a scaffold, firm and reliable, able to bear weight. Let your life move through it like a river, generous and sustaining to every bank it reaches. A man who is truthful but not generous becomes a statue in a graveyard. A man who is generous but not truthful becomes a mirage in the heat.

Be both. Be the structure that supports and the flow that sustains. In doing so, you do not just acquire wealth; you become a source of it for everyone who crosses your path.

◆ ◆ ◆

A generous liar builds cages with golden bars.
A truthful miser builds a fortress with no door.
One trades in illusion.
The other starves in his own certainty.

THE UNFORCED WAY

On Surrender and the Shadow

We hold the reins of our lives with a white-knuckled grip, convinced that if we let go, the world will dissolve into chaos. We cling to control because it is our most convincing mask for safety. When the tide turns against us, our instinct is rarely to understand the current; it is to command the water: *Stop. Change. Be what I need you to be.*

Look closer and it becomes clear that we are not trying to control the external event. We are trying to control the storm it awakens within us, the sudden feeling of being small, disrespected, or unsafe.

Imagine someone wounds you with a sharp word. The heat rises, a physical fire in your chest. You argue, you litigate, you marshal evidence to prove your righteousness. In that moment, you are trying to manipulate their perception to soothe your own internal bleeding. You are attempting to rewrite reality so you don't have to feel the pain of the wound.

Now, imagine the person across from you possesses the quiet wealths we have explored: a **Steady Mind**, unshaken by your tempests; a **Strength** rooted in presence rather than volume; and the **Wisdom** to know that some fires are not meant to be fought, but simply left to burn out. They refuse to enter the arena you've built. By standing still, they expose your struggle for what it truly is: a battle not with them, but with your own inability to hold your own hurt.

You cannot command a volcano to cease its eruption. You can only learn to read the tremors and step out of the path of the flow. This is not a surrender of power; it is the profound intelligence of nature. You do not ask the fire to be water. You recognize its nature, and you act accordingly.

The Crow in the Daylight

We are often taught that "evil" is an external monster, a shadow lurking in the dark. But why is divinity always associated with the sun, and the devil with the night?

Consider a crow that is ashamed of its own color. In the brilliant, unforgiving daylight, it feels exposed and judged. So, it hides, venturing out only in the dusk where its black feathers blend into the gloom. Its shame dictates the boundaries of its world.

Now consider a man who carries hidden shame, a belief that he is unworthy, ineloquent, or not enough. He fears the stage of life, the open light of honest connection. He retreats into sarcasm, silence, or subtle manipulation. Indirectness becomes his refuge, because directness feels unbearable.

The "devil" in our lives is rarely a monster from the outside. It is the collection of unloved, unacknowledged parts of ourselves that we have forced into the darkness: the bitterness we mask as "realism," the envy we dress up as critique, the fear we call "logic." We hide these things, and from that hidden place, we try to control the world around us just to ensure no one ever turns on the lights.

Evil is not what attacks you from the dark; it is what you choose to hide from the light.

A truly powerful man, one who cultivates his inner wealth, begins by bringing his crows into the daylight. He acknowledges shame and inadequacy. He looks at their color and says, "This too is mine." This is the ground of **truthfulness**. When you stop hiding from yourself, the urge to control others loosens its grip.

The Curriculum of Destruction

Life has a relentless, beautiful curriculum designed to bring your crows into the light. It achieves this by presenting you with exactly what you feel you cannot sacrifice.

I learned this through the slow accumulation of silence. As a child, I wanted a toy; my parents said no. I wanted a sweet; they said no. A pattern took root in my young heart: *Desire leads only to rejection.* To protect myself, I performed a pre-emptive strike: I stopped wanting. I would see something beautiful and instantly snuff out the spark of "I like that." Don't ask, and you won't be hurt.

This was the birth of a silent, self-imposed poverty. I wasn't practicing discipline; I was practicing fear. The sacrifices grew: the bicycle I never asked for, the career path I never voiced, the love I never pursued. I was building a life on the foundation of *"I do not deserve to be heard."*

But the universe has a way of identifying the one thing you cannot sacrifice—the one desire that burns too brightly to be extinguished by an old story. It might be a person, a mission, or a sense of freedom. This desire becomes the fulcrum. To have it, you must destroy the cage you built. You must stand in the daylight, voice your "I want," and face the potential "no" without crumbling.

The creation uses your deepest wants to dismantle your oldest defenses. It feels like chaos, like loss, like a demolition. But it is always a demolition for the sake of renovation.

The Practice of Active Surrender

This is the ultimate surrender: to stop trying to edit the external story and submit to the internal curriculum. It is the realization that painful and unexpected events are not random punishments; they are precise tools meant to break your specific chains.

This is not passive resignation. It is active surrender, the conscious choice to meet reality as it is, not as you wish it to be. It calls upon every form of wealth you are building:

- **A Steady Mind** to witness the breaking without becoming the drama.
- **Strength** to bear the collapse of your old forms.
- **Truthfulness** to admit what you truly want and what you truly fear.
- **Justice** to stop manipulating others to soothe your hidden shame.

The plan is not to make you comfortable; it is to make you whole. Your job is not to decode the grand design of the stars, but to tend to your own light. When you bring your crows into the sun, you stop shouting at volcanoes. You learn to move with the tremors. You discover that the sunlight was never your enemy; it was the only thing capable of showing you your true, unashamed colors.

Surrender is not about losing control. It is about transferring your trust from your fragile plans to your emerging, unbreakable strength. It is the final, fearless step toward becoming a man who cannot be manipulated—even by his own oldest fears.

◆◆◆

Stop shouting at volcanoes.
Learn to read the tremors instead.
You cannot stop the eruption
but you can choose not to build your house in the ash.

JUDGMENT IS NOT CLARITY

By now, you have been building a form of wealth that does not rely on approval or applause. It is built through discipline, through honoring your word, and through character shaped in silence. What you are carrying forward is not fragile. It is earned.

But as the structure of a man grows taller, a hidden pressure begins to mount. There is a silent force that can corrode even the strongest inner sanctum. It does not announce itself as an enemy; it arrives wearing the mask of intelligence, the heavy robes of experience, and the stern face of "being realistic."

That force is Judgment.

Judgment feels like clarity. It offers the seductive comfort of certainty. It leans close and whispers, "I have seen this pattern before. I know exactly how this story ends." It promises to protect you, assuring you that by categorizing the world, you can never truly be hurt by it. But judgment is a deceptive guardian. **Judgment is memory pretending to be truth.** It is the moment you stop seeing the living, breathing human in front of you and begin reacting to a shadow cast by your own past.

To truly dismantle this habit, we must look to the one whom the ancient Tamizh tradition called Naathan, the Great One: **Shiva.**

The Paradox of the Boon-Giver

(This section discusses Hindu religious ideas. Readers may approach it thoughtfully or skip it if they wish.)

To the casual eye, Shiva appears as a contradiction. He is the supreme ascetic, seated in the icy silence of the forest, draped in the ash of the dead. Yet he is Mahadeva, the source of all power. He is the destroyer of worlds, and still he is known as Ashutosh, the one who is easily pleased and generous with boons.

In the old stories, a demon often performs a terrible, singular penance. Shiva appears and asks, "*What do you seek?*" The demon asks for power, often the power to dominate or to escape the natural cycle of death. And Shiva grants it.

The result is almost always chaos. Another force must eventually intervene to restore balance. As children, we hear this and feel a sense of protest. "*Why give power to evil? Was he blind? Was he careless?*" It takes a lifetime to realize that the lesson was never in the destruction that followed.

The lesson lives in the sacred vacancy of the moment of the asking.

The Moment Before Memory: The Ash of the Past

When a being stands before Shiva in deep penance, Shiva does not consult a cosmic tax ledger. He does not tally past crimes or calculate future risks. He wears ash on his body as a reminder: the past is already burnt. It is gone.

In that moment of prayer, Shiva sees only one thing: a being fully present, fully focused, and stripped of distraction. He sees a soul in a state of supreme capability. To deny the boon based on what the being was would be to chain the present to the past. It would be Shiva saying, "*Your history has permanently defined you. You are incapable of evolution.*" If Shiva judged, he would cease to be Divinity and become a Bureaucrat of Fear. Shiva's act says something radical: "*I will meet you in your present. I will honor your effort, not my fear of your history. What you do with the gift is your karma; my duty is to be true to the principle that sincere seeking must be rewarded.*" He gives the boon to the Devotion, not the demon. This is the highest form of masculine consciousness: the ability to respond to the raw reality of the now, unclouded by the ghosts of memory.

The Tyranny of Transferred Memory

What Shiva refuses to do, we do habitually.

Day after day, We take our old, unhealed wounds, project them onto the fresh faces of those we love, and tragedy of tragedies, we call this "experience."

This pattern rarely announces itself as cruelty. It is far more insidious because it hides inside our virtues. It wears the costume of care, protection, and hard-won experience. Parents, partners, and leaders rarely intend to diminish the people they lead. But they lack the clarity to see the difference between a current danger and a past scar.

Their warnings are rarely about you. They are echoes of a fear that once kept them alive.

The Ghosts We Carry

Consider the ordinary heartbreaks of daily life.

Picture a manager who hovers, scolds, and micromanages your every move. It feels personal. A direct judgment of your competence. But look closer. Before you ever walked through that door, he trusted someone who failed him. That betrayal cut deep, and the memory hardened into a need for control. When he looks at you, he doesn't see your potential; he sees the echo of that past failure. He isn't managing you; he is managing his own unresolved anxiety.

Or imagine a father who once witnessed a terrible accident. Years later, you tell him you want to race. He forbids it. Is he protecting you? Yes. But he is also desperately trying to stop a movie playing in his head A scene where he felt utterly powerless. He isn't judging your skill; he is judging the future through a single, terrifying snapshot from his past.

We see this mechanism most painfully in love. Imagine your heart was once broken by someone you trusted explicitly. Fear became your survival mechanism. Years later, you meet someone who genuinely adores you. But instead of letting love in, suspicion arrives first. You assume the betrayal is inevitable. You question their motives; you monitor their choices.

Your partner may be innocent, devoted, and true, yet you force them to stand trial for crimes committed by an ex-lover years ago. This isn't discernment. It is a disrespect towards them, born of trauma.

A man who never learned to stand his ground sees a younger soul preparing for a challenge. "Don't go," he warns. "It's too dangerous." He thinks he is being sensible. In truth, he is exporting his own retreat. He is limiting someone else's potential based on his own remembered defeat.

There are endless examples, We do this to society. e look at someone from a troubled background and quietly decide their future before they've even lived it. We deny them their own hero's journey because we are too busy judging them by a statistic.

We think judgment keeps us safe. In reality, it only keeps us small. It trades the vast possibility of the now for a cramped prison built entirely of memory.

The Cost of Being Right

When you judge, you remove yourself from the flow of life and place yourself above it. You become the sole judge in a courtroom of one, surrounded by categories instead of human connections. You might be "right" about someone's flaws, but being correct is a cold, poor substitute for being understood.

A person who judges loses their fluidity, an open heart to receive.

Inner stability isn't just about you feeling good. It is about having the strength to grant freedom to everyone around you. Stop imposing your history onto the present. Meet the world as it is. Honor the effort. Release the outcome.

Power of meditation

Ancient sages emphasized meditation not just for peace, but for internal hygiene. It is the act of wiping the mud off the windshield of your mind. You must consciously remind yourself each morning: The person I meet today is not the ghost that wounded me yesterday.

A Note to the Reader: This book is not a spiritual manual, and I will not dive into the deeper mechanics of meditative states here. I could explain them in great detail, but doing so would assume you are not capable of exploring them yourself. As we have just discussed, I am trying to step away from judging anyone's capacity. I will leave the deeper exploration to you. I trust that you can handle the water.

◆◆◆

The highest form of masculinity is not domination.
It is liberation
first of yourself from the prison of memory,
then of others from the sentence of your judgment.

THE SACRED UNION

On Sex, Symbols

The inner landscapes of the soul demand care. Character must be tended, vows guarded, weight earned. Yet a conscious life is never lived in isolation. Each of us is born into a stream, an ancient and thundering river of symbols, stories, and archetypal rituals carried forward by those who breathed before us.

To be a conscious man today is to act as a **translator** of that river. It is the arduous, beautiful task of separating the eternal, crystalline meaning from the temporary mud of superstition. We must recover the map without mistaking the aging paper for the land itself.

Every civilization, in its peak of wisdom, has attempted to describe the same core pulse of reality using different dialects. They all arrived at a singular realization: **Creation requires two forces.** One that is profoundly still, and one that is perpetually moving. Remove the stillness, and motion becomes a chaotic storm. Remove the motion, and stillness becomes the rot of decay. This is not mere theology; it is the fundamental physics of the spirit. It is the axis and the wheel. The screen and the cinematic light. Awareness and Action.

The Shivalingam – The Sacred Geometry of Origin

(This section discusses Hindu religious ideas. Readers may approach it thoughtfully or skip it if they wish.)

To the uninitiated eye, the Shivalingam is reduced to stone, or worse, misread through a narrow modern lens of biology. This is a failure of depth, a literalism that cannot see the poetry of the cosmos.

The Shivalingam is not an idol to be stared at; it is a **cosmic metaphor** to be understood. It represents the primordial union of the Masculine principle (Shiva, pure Consciousness) and the Feminine principle (Shakti, Creative Energy). It is the exact point where stillness meets dynamism, the friction-less pivot from which the entire universe unfurls.

On a human scale, this points to the visceral truth of our own beginning. The union of man and woman is the mirror of that cosmic dance. From this union emerges the ultimate mystery: a new soul, a new breath, a new possibility.

The Poverty of the "Flex"

This is why intimacy was traditionally held as sacred. Not because the ancients were "prudes" who viewed the body as a sin, but because they viewed it as a **solemn responsibility.** The act that possesses the power to call a soul into existence is not a game.

To treat this power as casual currency, to use intimacy for validation or to boast of conquests, is ignorance, plain and costly. It does not display strength. It reveals inner poverty. A ritual meant for the sanctum is dragged into the marketplace. It is like using sacred scripture to wrap fish.

A man of true wealth understands that strength is shown not in display, but in reverence. In restraint. In the careful stewardship of what has the power to give life.

The Karuvarai – The Sanctum and the Womb

The architectural genius of the ancient Tamizh temple reveals a psychological secret. The innermost sanctum, the dark, silent heart where the deity resides, is called the Karuvarai. In the Tamizh language, this word has a double resonance: it also means **Womb**.

The message carved into the very stone of our history is clear: the divine is not a distant, external entity. The potential for the divine is encoded within the very act of bringing life into the world. The womb is the first temple; the temple is a symbolic womb. To disrespect the creative power of the feminine is to desecrate the heart of the temple. A conscious man protects this sacredness not through control, but through honor. He understands that some covenants are meant to be private, and their value lies in their depth, not their visibility.

The River and The Fire – A Manual for the Soul

Our ancestors were master psychologists. They understood the human mind as a landscape that needs constant care, a place where clutter gathers and impurities can settle. They did not merely worship the elements. They used them as living metaphors for mental hygiene. Dissolving in the river and burning in the fire were not literal acts, but inner processes, ways of releasing what could not be carried and transforming what could not remain.

They taught us: **Use the river in your mind to release. Use the fire in your will to transform.**

1. The River: The Flow of Conscious Release

The Metaphor: A river cleans itself through movement. Its nature is flow. Silt is carried away, and the source remains alive. You cannot hold a river still, just as you cannot cling to a mistake without inviting stagnation.

When to use this metaphor: For lapses of character. A sharp word spoken in anger. A moment of petty jealousy. A minor promise left unkept. These are the silt of daily life.

The Mental Ritual (How to "use the river" in your mind):

Do not build a dam of guilt. Guilt is stagnant water; it breeds resentment and self-pity. Instead:

- **Acknowledge the fault.** See it clearly. Feel its weight.
- **Place it in the river of your conscious awareness.** Visualize the flow of your forward-moving life, your better intentions, your core values.
- **Let the flow carry it.** Do not clutch it. The lesson can remain on the bank. The shame, the replaying, the weight do not need to come with you. Allow the current of the mind to move them downstream, out of your immediate life. You are not the mistake. You are the water that knows how to move past it.

2. The Fire: The Heat of Transformation

The Metaphor: Fire doesn't just move; it fundamentally changes what it touches. It turns dense wood into weightless ash and soft ore into hardened steel. It is the agent of alchemy.

When to use this metaphor: For foundational flaws. Deep habits of deceit. Entitlement. Corrosive bitterness. These cannot be released and left intact. They would poison the inner stream. They must be broken down and remade.

The Mental Ritual (How to "use the fire" in your mind):

This requires the fierce, disciplined heat of uncompromising self-inquiry.

1. **Gather the flaw.** Identify it with ruthless honesty.

2. **Submit it to the fire of your conscious will.** This means sitting in the discomfort of examining it. Why does it exist? What fear or lack does it come from? Shine the relentless light of your awareness on it.
3. **Hold it there until it transforms.** The fire is sustained commitment. Justification burns. The pattern loosens. The identity tied to the flaw is consumed. What remains is not ash, but essence. Strength forged from jealousy overcome. Integrity born from deceit burned away.

3. In Essence: A Practice for the Inner World

The sage's instruction was never to literally throw objects into physical elements. It was always a call to internal action:

1. **To "dissolve in the river" is to practice non-attachment to past errors.** It is the mental act of forgiveness (of self and others) and conscious release.
2. **To "burn in the fire" is to practice radical self-accountability.** It is the mental act of confronting, breaking down, and rebuilding the parts of your character that hold you back.

These are the timeless tools: **the flowing water of release** for the dirt that settles daily, and the **focused fire of will for the deep impurities** that have hardened within. Use them to tend the landscape of your mind.

The Duty of the Conscious Man

We live in a fractured time. We stand between two failures: the outsider who mocks these symbols out of a lack of depth, and the insider who performs them as empty, superstitious theater. The conscious man must walk the narrow, difficult ridge between them.

He does not perform rituals for show; he lives their meaning.

- When he looks at the Shivalingam, he sees the awe of existence and makes his relationships a sanctuary, not a trophy room.

- When he encounters the "River and the Fire," he looks inward. He practices the grace of the river for his errors and the ferocity of the fire for his evolution.

The river flows. The fire burns. The union creates. Your life is the stage where these ancient metaphors must finally become real. Do not let the stories stay in the books or the stone. Let them breathe through your actions.

Make your life worthy of the meaning it carries.

◆ ◆ ◆

Do not worship the idol.
Worship the principle it points to.
Do not perform the ritual.
Live the truth it teaches.
The map is not the land.

THE BREATH OF A CONSCIOUS LIFE

Freedom

At some point, every life encounters a tightening. It does not arrive loudly or all at once. It gathers quietly, behind the ribs, narrowing choice, voice, even breath. This is not a modern inconvenience. It is an ancient signal, the soul's memory pressing for release.

In Indian thought, this release is called Moksha (liberation). It is often misunderstood as a distant, mystical escape. Moksha is not withdrawal from the world, but freedom within it. It is a way of living here and now, awake, clear, and unburdened, not a reward deferred until after death.

Many paths point toward this horizon: **Dhyaana (meditation), Bhakti (devotion), and Karma (right action).** The ancient Tamizh tradition, however, followed a way of life in which all of these were held together. Liberation was not something to be theorized; it had to be lived. Philosophy without habit is merely decoration, a coat of paint on a crumbling wall. If freedom is the aim, it must be made ordinary. It must be woven into Tuesday afternoons and difficult conversations.

The Daily Sharpening of the Inner Sword

A man's greatest weapon is not muscle, but consciousness. Like any blade, it dulls when neglected. To wield it well, one must see clearly, without the fog of self-flattery, why one acts as one does.

Meditation is not an escape from reality. It is the daily sharpening of the inner blade. It asks you to sit still long enough to watch the machinery of your own mind at work. Thoughts rise and fall like waves. With practice, they lose their authority. You begin to sense the crucial difference between a **thought and a command.** In the pause between stimulus and response, freedom first appears.

Without that pause, you are a puppet. You mistake old, knee-jerk reactions for "thinking" and call them "decisions." Meditation gives you the power to choose otherwise. It grants you the sovereignty of your own mind.

Riverbanks: The Architecture of Force

There is a crucial truth that many seekers miss: **Freedom without boundaries is not liberation; it is chaos**. A river without banks cannot flow; it simply spreads thin and vanishes into the mud. Your boundaries are not cages meant to trap you; they are the riverbanks that allow your force to gather, move, and eventually reach the sea.

To live the "Sixteen Wealths" is to define who you are and, more importantly, what you will refuse. If you possess every form of external wealth yet numb your soul with drink the moment pain arrives, you reveal the brokenness beneath the display. The problem is not the drink; the problem is the flight from the work of consciousness. True freedom is not the license to "do anything." It is the strength to do what is right when it is grueling, and the clarity to know the difference.

The Trap of the Proxy: Freedom's Hardest Test

Freedom is an easy concept when the enemy is a stranger in the street. It becomes a harrowing ordeal when the enemy uses a face you love.

A manipulative world knows it cannot break a strong man directly. If a stranger orders you to surrender your dignity, you will refuse. You will fight. So the world plays a smarter, more subtle game: The Proxy. The forces that wish to control you will not attack you directly; they will manipulate your parents, your elders, or the "peace-keepers" in your family. They will convince the people you love that your compliance is "necessary" for the family's honor or "good" for your future.

Now the pressure no longer comes from a villain. It comes from a mother or a father. *"Do this for us. Don't cause trouble. Just adjust."* If you yield to that weight, who truly wins? Not your parents. They were only the instrument. The one who wins is the force behind the curtain that thrives on compliance.

The Courage of Disagreement

Will you oppose those you love on this? Yes. If you seek Truth (Satyam) and Justice (Aram), you must. We are often taught that respect is synonymous with silence. This is a lie.

- **Silence** when a loved one is being manipulated is not respect; it is negligence.
- **Agreement** when an elder is fundamentally wrong is not obedience; it is cowardice.

A relationship with your parents or spouse is not a hierarchy where you must shrink to appease them. It is a **Circle of Truth.** If they are wrong, argue. Fight for the truth. Get clarified. Put the hard reality on the table. Friction creates fire, and fire creates light. Wisdom reaches us not through passive nodding, but in the heat of honest, sometimes painful exchange. If they refuse to understand, if they insist on being the proxy for someone else's game, then Justice demands that you reject the demand and move forward alone. You protect the relationship by refusing to let it be used as a tool for manipulation.

The Manual of the Liberated Life

This is not "holy" work; it is practical work. Here are the habits that make freedom a tangible reality:

1. **The Daily Sit:** Start with ten minutes. Watch your breath. Do not fight your thoughts; let them move like traffic on a distant street. This is not about emptying the mind, but about making space. That daily reset expands the "pause" between impulse and action.

2. **Audit your borders:** Write down what you will no longer tolerate, from others and, more importantly, from yourself. Ask whether each boundary is born of fear or of dignity. *"I will never trust again"* is a prison. *"I will not tolerate being lied to"* is a bridge to freedom.

3. **Service Without a Ledger:** Once a week, perform one act of service with no expectation of thanks or return. Observe the shift inside you. Freedom is not total independence; it is the skill of selfless exchange.

4. **Name the Old Tapes:** When a surge of anger, shame, or panic rises, ask: *"Which old tape is playing?"* When you name it aloud, the tape loses its power. It becomes a sound, not a command.

5. **The Rise after the Fall:** You will miss your sessions. You will cross a boundary you swore to protect. This is data, not doom. Note the trigger, learn from the sting, and stand up again. The courage to stand repeatedly is the very essence of manhood.

The Final Mirror

Moksha is not a reward waiting at the end of a life. It is a **quality** brought to this breath. It appears when action and truth align, when life is lived from the center of clarity rather than the edges of habit.

You are both the river and the bank, the seeker and the path. Start where you are. Sit. Breathe. Write down one boundary and honor it for a single week. Keep one small, seemingly insignificant promise to yourself.

Freedom is never given. It is built, one conscious breath, one honest word, one courageous step at a time. It costs nothing, yet it demands everything. It is the final wealth, the liberty to live as you were meant to live, unbought, unbowed, and awake.

◆ ◆ ◆

Your greatest weapon is not strength, but consciousness.
Meditation sharpens the blade of awareness
the space between a thought and your action
is where your freedom lives.

THE RETURN TO LIFE

On Greatness & Integrated Life

This book opened before a mirror. What followed was not a straight path, but a demanding one. Shame had to be faced without flinching. Debt had to be named for what it was. Grief had to be entered, not bypassed. Along the way, brotherhood took shape, the sanctity of one's word was brought under governance, and the weighty responsibility of raising the next generation came fully into view.

You have gathered the wealths. You have the tools hanging heavy and ready on your belt. But we must be honest with one another: a tool belt does not make a carpenter, and a map, no matter how beautifully drawn, is not the journey itself.

Now comes the hardest part, the part where the theory ends and the living begins.

The Hero's Homecoming: The Temple and the Marketplace

Every soul moves through inevitable stages: survival, pleasure, the hunger for comfort, and the search for respect. Eventually, the compass needle of a man's life begins to swing inward toward love, meditation, and higher consciousness.

There is a quiet beauty in this progression. If comfort or recognition calls to you, do not suppress it. Ensure that the desire rises from your own depth, not from a script handed down by others. **That is sovereignty.**

Yet the journey does not end with the discovery of treasure in a dark cave. It ends when that treasure is carried back home, into the noisy, imperfect village that was once left behind.

It is easy to be holy on a mountain. It is easy to feel "zen" in the silent aisles of a library or while reading a book about righteousness in a quiet room. But you do not live on a mountain. You live in the grinding gears of traffic. You live in the sharp-edged politics of the office. You live in the relentless noise of family demands, unexpected bills, and the friction of a world that refuses to slow down for your peace.

You might ask, *"I have changed, so why hasn't the world?"* The traffic is still loud. Corruption still casts its shadow. People are still rushing, blind to their own breath. But remember this: the mountain did not get smaller; **your legs simply got stronger.** You did not build your Internal Fortress to hide inside it. You built it so you could walk through the fire without the smell of smoke ever clinging to your clothes.

The Brick and the Battle: A Soldier's Confession

Do not fall into the trap of thinking you must transform into this man overnight. Just because you now understand the path does not mean your feet won't stumble. If you try to rewrite your entire existence today, your body and mind will rebel. They will feel the weight of perfection as a crushing burden.

A cathedral is built brick by single brick. Not in a day. Not in a month.

I wrote these words for you, but please, do not mistake me for a finished master standing on a distant pedestal. I have not achieved all of this perfectly. I am not a guru; I am a soldier in the same muddy trench as you. I am also trying. I am also fighting the daily, gritty war against my own lethargy and my own oldest fears. Life is about taking ownership of your senses and acting with freedom, rather than living within the cages we accidentally build for ourselves. Start slowly. Lay one brick of integrity today. Lay another tomorrow. That is the only way a man truly rises.

The Symphony of the Whole Drum: Beyond Division

Before parting, one final conflict must be addressed: the conflict of division. In the ancient traditions, it is said that all wisdom flowed from the Damaru, the small drum held by Shiva. When it was played, one side echoed with the sounds that became Sanskrit. The other side echoed with the sounds that became Tamizh.

Today, small minds fight over which side is "better." It is as foolish as arguing whether your left lung is superior to your right, or whether fire is more "truthful" than water. They are the two halves of a single, divine heartbeat:

- **Tamizh traditions** speak through the soul of Aram, the intuition of Nadi, the mystic Siddhar way, the healing of Siddha Vaithiyam, and the secret science of the breath, Vasi.
- **Sanskrit traditions** offer the structural depth of Dharma, the cosmic calculations of Jyotisha, the intricate weave of the Tantras, and the systemic wisdom of Ayurveda.

To reject one is to choose to be half a man. They are complementary paths to the same mountain peak. A conscious man does not choose sides in a perspective game; he listens to the **rhythm of the whole drum**. He honors the breath of both languages and gets complete.

(Rather than debating which language came first, it is better to preserve all languages, as each carries the wisdom of our ancestors.)

The Sixteenth Wealth: Greatness

In the Thirukkural, the sage Thiruvalluvar speaks of Perumai (Greatness). He defines it with a stunning, humanistic paradox: *"The nature of Greatness is humility. The nature of Smallness is to admire itself."*

This is the final, unwritten wealth: **Integration**. It is the moment when you stop trying to be a conscious man and simply are one. You no longer struggle to be truthful; you simply have no appetite for the taste of a lie. You don't "try" to be generous; your hand opens before your mind can even begin its calculations. You don't force yourself to be resilient; you flow like a river because you have finally forgotten how to be a stagnant pond.

The Final Call: Masculinity in Motion

The inner path has been walked. The steadying of the mind. The tending of the body as a temple. But this was never an escape. **It was preparation.** The world is not a meditation hall. It is a field where silence, when misplaced, becomes complicity.

You have gathered the sixteen wealths, but a man does not hoard his peace. He deploys it. He does not just guard his strength; he stands between harm and those who cannot stand alone. He plants his integrity like a boundary stone and declares that here, no corruption shall pass. This is masculinity in motion.

Look around you. Protection is found in the ordinary, honest act: the merchant who refuses to cheat for profit, the professional who speaks up when a shortcut is taken, or the father who says "enough" to a debt that would enslave his children's future. These are the choices of a man who cannot be bought.

Take these sixteen wealths out of these pages and carry them into the boardrooms, the streets, and the quiet, heavy moments of choice. You did the inner work so that when the time comes to protect, you will be unmovable. Go now—not in anger, but in clarity. Not for glory, but for the good. The true masculine does not dominate; it protects. It does not perform; it preserves.

Maintaining all of this is difficult. It is an everyday struggle. Failure is frequent. I fail often, and I am still trying. Evolution from one form to another is never easy. That is the truth.

A world shaped by righteous people would not feel like a conquest or a performance; it would feel calm. We would share without counting, grow without comparison, and let our desires breathe without turning them into proof. When men and women no longer need to justify their worth to one another, judgment loosens, hearts soften, and life grows lighter. Not because the world was repaired, but because we finally learned how to live beside one another without fear.

If anything in this book has stirred a quiet knowing in you, perhaps it is because that knowing was already there, waiting to be remembered.

THE WORLD IS WAITING FOR US!!!

ABOUT THE AUTHOR

***Siva Murugan**, traditionally known as "Magam Thirunal Siva Murugan," is an independent thinker concerned with how modern life shapes character, conflict, choice, and consequence, focusing on the man who senses there is more to life than income and image. He invites a return to a masculinity grounded in self-mastery rather than domination.*

By drawing from the lived knowledge of his ancestors and the ethical traditions of Tamizh culture, he seeks to share an older understanding of life. This perspective is rooted in responsibility, restraint, and inner steadiness. His work reflects a deep awareness that societies are not fixed through shortcuts or loud solutions. Instead, they are built by patient, disciplined individuals who take full ownership of their actions.

He does not write to reform the world overnight. His focus remains on clarity over speed, responsibility over convenience, and the long work of building character in a time preoccupied with performance. His writing is grounded, deliberate, and driven by the belief that meaningful change begins with the individual and unfolds naturally over time.

If you find this meaningful, I've shared a few more short writings on my site. Please feel free to visit.

www.sivamurugan.co.in

For the Curious Readers: Sources of Inspiration

This book is a reflection on living wisdom, not an academic study. Its voice is shaped by the unseen currents of Tamizh thought, the quiet teachings of my ancestors, and the raw material of lived experience.

For those who wish to walk further into the forest from which these ideas sprang, here are a few of the timeless texts and traditions that have been my companions:

- **Thirukkural** – The classic Tamizh treatise on virtue, wealth, and love, composed by Thiruvalluvar. Its verses on aram (righteousness), porul (wealth), and inbam (joy) gently map the geography of a conscious life.
- **Tholkappiyam** – The ancient Tamizh grammar and work on poetics that also deeply explores the inner and outer worlds (akam and puram), human emotions, and the ethics of living in harmony with nature and society.
- **Purananuru & Agananuru** – Sangam-era anthologies that capture the spirit, courage, ethics, and daily life of ancient Tamizhakam. They teach through story, song, and stark human truth.
- The rich tradition of **Tamizh Saiva literature**, including the poetic works on Sivan, Murugan, and the countless village deities who embody the interplay of nature, culture, and consciousness.
- The living oral tradition of **Tamizh proverbs, folklore, and family wisdom** which is often carried in the speech of grandparents, the rhythms of rituals, and the unspoken rules of hospitality and honor.

These are not meant to be studied, but felt. They are less about information and more about resonance. A way of seeing, weighing, and walking through the world.

9 789356 598935

Printed by Libri Plureos GmbH in Hamburg,
Germany